STANDING WITH THE VULNERABLE

A CURRICULUM FOR TRANSFORMING LIVES AND COMMUNITIES

Gil Odendaal

D1308031

IVP Connect

An imprint of InterVarsity Press
Downers Grove, Illinois

InterVarsity Press
P.O. Box 1400, Downers Grove, IL 60515-1426
ivpress.com
email@ivpress.com

InterVarsity Press® is the book-publishing division of InterVarsity Christian Fellowship/USA®, a movement of students and faculty active on campus at hundreds of universities, colleges and schools of nursing in the United States of America, and a member movement of the International Fellowship of Evangelical Students. For information about local and regional activities, visit intervarsity.org.

All Scripture quotations, unless otherwise indicated, are taken from THE HOLY BIBLE, NEW INTERNATIONAL VERSION®, NIV® Copyright © 1973, 1978, 1984, 2011 by Biblica, Inc.™ Used by permission. All rights reserved worldwide.

While any stories in this book are true, some names and identifying information may have been changed to protect the privacy of individuals.

Cover design: Cindy Kiple
Interior design: Beth McGill
Images: hands: Vectorig/iStockphoto
*   tree illustration: © Alex Belomlinksy/iStockphoto*

ISBN 978-0-8308-2099-3 (print)
ISBN 978-0-8308-9409-3 (digital)

Printed in the United States of America ♾

g green press As a member of the Green Press Initiative, InterVarsity Press is committed to protecting the environment and to the responsible
INITIATIVE use of natural resources. To learn more, visit greenpressinitiative.org.

Library of Congress Cataloging-in-Publication Data
A catalog record for this book is available from the Library of Congress.

P	24	23	22	21	20	19	18	17	16	15	14	13	12	11	10	9	8	7	6	5	4	3	2	1
Y	37	36	35	34	33	32	31	30	29	28	27	26	25	24	23	22	21	20	19	18	17	16		

To Elmarie, my closest friend, soul mate, and wife, who
through personal sacrifice, selflessness, and without material reward
but with undivided love, devotion, sacrifice, and assistance freely given
enabled me to complete this book, and without whose support
I would never have been able to continue on my life journey
and the race Christ has placed before me

"Engaging our communities and the world with the practical love of Christ has always been the church's mandate but never an easy task to accomplish. No one is better qualified than Dr. Odendaal to reignite our vision and practice of loving God and our neighbor. It's hard to imagine a more insightful, experienced, and biblically grounded guide."

Duane Elmer, G. W. Alden Professor of International Studies (retired), Trinity International University, author of *Cross-Cultural Servanthood*

"Anyone who reads the Gospels with an open mind can hardly miss the fact that the God who became a man in Jesus Christ was, and still continues to be, especially concerned for the vulnerable. Gil Odendaal provides valuable practical help to people who are really serious in their commitment to follow Jesus by standing with the vulnerable in their own situation today."

René Padilla, emeritus president, The Kairos Foundation, executive director, Ediciones Kairos

"If you are planning to go to communities in the Global South for missional purposes, this book will help you gain a deeper understanding of the human needs there, but the change theory used throughout this study is equally applicable to the church in North America. World Relief has used it in Africa and Asia, resulting in vibrant local congregations impacting their communities in word and deed. Now you have an opportunity to experience that impact in your own life and the life of your church."

Stephan Bauman, executive director, Cornerstone Trust, previously president of World Relief

"Gil's book provides a biblical, crosscultural, and practical resource to help transform God's people to understand the whole gospel of Jesus for the whole person, helping them be an equipped church that experiences and expresses God's heart for those who are caught in vulnerable places and need a touch of God's love."

Timothy Ek, development officer, The LIGHT House, Lee's Summit, Missouri, former vice president, The Evangelical Covenant Church

"Pastors whose hearts beat for the nations and the display of God's glory will love this insightful and practical resource to guide their churches to be better equipped in long-term transformational mission strategies and practices. *Standing with the Vulnerable* is a kingdom-minded resource for global-minded people. Many churches have a desire to have a global gospel footprint but lack the strategic insight to accomplish it. Gil Odendaal's love for the nations and for the church has forged a resource that is greatly helpful to both, and it will prove to be an effective resource for community transformation."

Randy Gunter, senior pastor, MeadowBrook Baptist Church, Gadsden, Alabama

"We often feel the world's problems are so overwhelming and so distant to us that there is little we can contribute. In this great study, Dr. Gil Odendaal takes us on a journey into Scripture, into a needy world, and into our own hearts. We see that the principles we need for personal growth and transformation are the very same truths that enable us to be part of God's life-bringing mission. The material is easy to read, but don't be fooled; there is much here that draws on the best understanding of mission and development. Be transformed!"

Paul Bendor-Samuel, executive director, Oxford Centre for Mission Studies

"Gil Odendaal is a leader, an author, a pastor, and a shepherd to so many. 'Standing with the vulnerable' is arguably the best description one could make about Gil. His passion and love for the Lord shine through in so many ways, and his desire to seek and to serve are obviously evident in all he does. This Bible study will challenge you, encourage you, enhance your understanding of who the vulnerable are, and push you to further explore how best to stand in the gap with and for the least of these."

Charles D. Sands, PhD provost and vice president for academic affairs, California Baptist University, Riverside

"Gil's work in *Standing with the Vulnerable* is fantastic. There is a significant void today for resources that help us better understand proper philosophies of engagement for global relief and development. Recent experiences have shown us so much of the damage that can be done when founded improperly, but few have come to bear the burden of a solution. Gil is masterful in this work, carefully guiding the reader through the fundamental principles while also providing the opportunity to digest the thoughts and unpack what they mean to you."

Will Rogers, executive director, Global Medical Health Conference, founder, X362: World's First Vision Achievement Platform

"I have been privileged to know Gil Odendaal as a friend and colleague and to observe the highly influential role he has played as an ambassador for the poor and a cutting-edge leader in the integral mission movement, within the relief and development context. He brings a rare combination of academic knowledge, practical experience, and a gracious and humble spirit. But it is his heart that impresses me the most, and that clearly comes through in all that he does. I heartily commend this book to you and feel that Gil is uniquely qualified to speak into these issues in a practical way that truly enables people to put love into action."

Tom Watkins, director of strategic initiatives and partnerships, Trans World Radio

"*Standing with the Vulnerable* makes the case that poverty is more than a physical circumstance and its solution is deeper than material possessions. Spiritual poverty cannot be ignored, and we as Christ-followers have the unique opportunity—and responsibility—to bring holistic change to the world's poor. Odendaal walks us, step by step, through a plan giving us an understanding of poverty and effective action."

Chad Hayward, executive director, Accord Network

"Faith and obedience are never separated in the Bible. From cover to cover, Scripture underlines the importance of caring for the poor and vulnerable in society. *Standing with the Vulnerable* is a helpful study guide that walks through the why and how and equips the reader with examples from real life situations. This is an important resource for individuals, teams, and church groups to learn from, reflect on, and respond to together. We are thrilled that Gil Odendaal and World Relief have shared this with us all."

Sheryl Haw, international director, Micah Global

"I highly recommend this book for any church serious about being missional in today's world. This is an incredible resource to take your congregation or group deeper in their understanding of what Jesus meant when he proclaimed 'fullness of life.' Using engaging Bible studies and real-life examples, Odendaal helps unpack the good news of the gospel in ways that will both challenge and encourage Christians to see how their faith should shape their response to the issues facing our local and global communities. I think this book will transform the way your church responds to mission."

Matthew Maury, CEO, TEAR Australia

"*Standing with the Vulnerable* is a practical, biblical roadmap for releasing the fullness of the gospel in the lives of families and communities. The truth in this study combines thought leadership in development with the real-life experience of grassroots ministry from World Relief staff and volunteers around the world. I highly commend it to you."

Steve Moore, executive director, nexleader, formerly executive director of Missio Nexus

CONTENTS

INTRODUCTION

World Relief is a Christian organization whose mission is to empower the local church to serve the most vulnerable. In community with the local church, World Relief sees orphans, widows, refugees, and families devastated by natural disaster transformed physically, spiritually, and economically.

At World Relief, we believe that obedience to the Great Commission (Matthew 28:19-20) and the Greatest Commandment (Matthew 22:37-38) demands that ministry is seamlessly integrated with the spiritual, physical, emotional, and social well-being of those Christ commands us to minister to. This is the call of integral mission for the church: to follow Jesus in all aspects of life by expressing the gospel in who we are, what we say, and all we do. Thus integral mission praxis can only take place when our "being" as Christ-followers forms the foundation for our "saying" and "doing."

This study will expose you to the "Tree Curriculum" that has been used in Africa and Asia, resulting in vibrant local congregations impacting their communities in word and deed. The stories of Sarah and John and the other characters are composites of situations that World Relief confronts and experiences in the regions where we work. Those planning to go to communities in the Global South for missional purposes will gain a deeper understanding of the human needs there, but the change theory used throughout this study is equally applicable to any of the four continents—including North America—where this material was originally developed. Our hope is that you not only gain insight to the curriculum used in transformational ministry, but that through these sessions you are also transformed.

How to Use These Sessions

Here are some helpful hints as you work your way through *Standing with the Vulnerable*.

Pray. Before you begin reading each session, start with prayer. Ask God to help you as you encounter new concepts and contemplate taking action.

Keep a Bible nearby. Many of the Scripture passages are included, but you'll want to look up others.

Take your time. These lessons are challenging. Read through the entire lesson and answer every question, but don't rush!

Write it down. In addition to writing down your responses to questions, you can underline statements you agree with and write down your questions in the margins. The more you interact with these sessions, the more you'll learn.

Be prepared to meet with your group. Complete the session ahead of time so you are prepared to share what you are learning with your group. Chances are if you're finding some element challenging, you're not alone.

Our hope is that *Standing with the Vulnerable* will challenge you and spur you on to be an agent of transformation in your community.

one

UNDERSTANDING DEVELOPMENT

✔ Objectives

- Define development.
- Explore development of the whole person and apply it to everyday life.
- Examine God's call to love him and our neighbor.

Developing the Whole Person

Development describes the process of how people and communities grow and change over time. But how does this growth happen?

Think about our many needs.

1. What does a person need to simply stay alive—to *survive*?

2. What is required for a person to have the best possible life—to *flourish*?

We want people to flourish, and in order for that to happen we need to help them meet all of their needs. We can group these needs into different areas.

- **Physical** needs are the needs of our **bodies**. This includes things such as food, proper medicine, shelter, clean water, and safety. Our bodies need all of these things to be physically well.
- **Mental** needs are the needs of our **minds**. This includes our ability to think, learn, and solve problems. Mental needs include education in school. They also include

learning outside of school—learning from our experiences and people in our lives.

- **Emotional** needs are the needs of our **hearts**. Here we talk about the feeling part of us, what the Bible calls the "heart." We all need to know love, hope, and joy in our lives. When we are sad or angry, we need to be able to deal with these feelings in a helpful way. Emotional needs also include feeling good about who we are as individuals—having a positive view of ourselves.

- **Social** needs are the needs to have **relationships** with other people. We need to give and receive love and kindness. We need others to support us and care for us, and we help others by caring for them, too. This includes relationships with our families, friends, neighbors, and the community.

- We also have the need to **make good choices**. Unlike animals, people have the ability to think carefully before they act, to make choices, to plan ahead, and to determine how they will live their lives in the future. This includes making a choice and taking action to carry out the decision.

All people—men and women, infants and the elderly—have within them these areas of need. Take a look at your hand. Your five fingers can help you remember these five areas of development. But notice that your fingers aren't independent—they are connected to your palm. So as you look at your palm, think of your *spiritual life*. Just as your palm is connected to your fingers, every area of development is touched and controlled by your spiritual life. In other words, *every area of your life is spiritual*.

The apostle Paul talked about spiritual growth and development in his letter to the church in Corinth:

> I planted the seed, Apollos watered it, but God has been making it grow. So neither the one who plants nor the one who waters is anything, but only God, who makes things grow. The one who plants and the one who waters have one purpose, and they will each be rewarded according to their own labor. (1 Corinthians 3:6-8)

Development describes the process of how people and communities grow and change over time.

Spiritual development includes knowing and loving God and having a relationship with him. This can only happen by believing that he sent his son Jesus to die for your sins and asking him to forgive you and make you his child. But as you think about growth and development, remember that it is *only God* who makes things grow.

Once you have Jesus in your life, you can talk to him through prayer, worship him, and learn about him from reading the Bible and from others who also follow him. World Relief works to empower churches because the church is God's primary means to promote the spiritual growth of a person.

We all need many different things in order to grow into the people God intends us to be. But the spiritual part of us is like a light switch: when the switch is on it lights up the whole room. As you grow spiritually it has a positive influence on the other areas of your growth.

As you think of growth, imagine a small seed.

3. What does that seed need to grow?

> **Spiritual development includes knowing and loving God and having a relationship with him.**

4. What kinds of changes occur?

5. What does the seed become over time?

Aside from rain and sun, it takes *time* for a seed to become a tree and to produce fruits. Growth is a process.

We also want to see our families and our communities grow.

6. What hopes do you have for your family?

7. What changes do you hope will occur?

We have many dreams for the future. It is good to have dreams—they give us hope. By working together, we can help one another overcome difficulties and reach those dreams. We can help one another flourish.

Our *seeds* are our hopes for what will happen in the future. We want those seeds to grow and become real in our lives and in our communities.

Growing as a Whole Person

It is possible to be physically healed and yet still be plagued by emotional hurts when we are governed by false beliefs.

MR. MAFU

Mr. Mafu had a very nice bicycle. As he rode to work one day the bicycle hit a rock, causing Mr. Mafu to fall off and break his leg. His neighbor, a good friend, took him home and called the traditional healer. The healer said the neighbor brought this evil on Mr. Mafu. The healer also advised Mr. Mafu to go to the hospital. At the hospital the doctor put Mr. Mafu's leg into a plaster cast. Mr. Mafu kept saying, "It shows you cannot trust your best friend!" and thought of bad things he could do to his neighbor to pay back the evil his neighbor had done.

When Mr. Mafu returned to the hospital to have the plaster cast removed, he met a pastor there. He told the pastor his story, and the pastor said he should love his neighbor and even if that neighbor did curse him, Mr. Mafu should bless him instead. When the plaster came off, Mr. Mafu was very glad his leg was healed, but he decided to still do something bad to hurt his neighbor.

1. Was Mr. Mafu healed? Why or why not?

2. Why was Mr. Mafu's healing incomplete?

3. What can we learn from Mr. Mafu?

In our story, Mr. Mafu was not healthy even after his leg was healed. He was still angry and resentful, and he treated his neighbor badly. He will not be truly healed until he deals with these problems.

Growing well in all areas of our lives makes us more complete as people. And whole, complete people can contribute to healthy communities. In healthy communities everyone grows individually and together.

Growing and developing as children of God is not just about physical growth. It is about growing as a *whole* person. God created us with the need to develop physically, mentally, emotionally, and socially and the need to learn how to make good choices.

God's desire is that every human being attains well-being in all those areas. Each of these areas of our development connects to one another.

If one part improves, there will also be a positive benefit to another part.

4. If a child is well-fed, what other areas of that child's life are affected?

5. If a woman has a close relationship with God, what other areas of her life are affected?

6. If a child suffers physically and is hungry, what other areas of that child's life will suffer?

7. If a man suffers physically with HIV, what other areas of his life will suffer?

The Greatest Commandment

One day, an expert in the law asked Jesus a question:

> "Teacher," he asked, "what must I do to inherit eternal life?"
>
> "What is written in the Law?" [Jesus] replied. "How do you read it?"
>
> He answered, "'Love the Lord your God with all your heart and with all your soul and with all your strength and with all your mind'; and, 'Love your neighbor as yourself.'"
>
> "You have answered correctly," Jesus replied. "Do this and you will live." (Luke 10:25-28)

1. What areas of development are addressed here?

2. What do these verses tell you about how we should love God?

3. What do these verses tell you about how God sees our development?

4. The expert in the law asked what was the single most important commandment. Why do you think Jesus answered with the *two* most important commandments?

These two commands—to love God and love others—are the main things he wants from us. In other words, we cannot separate loving God from loving our neighbors. The Bible puts it this way:

> Whoever claims to love God yet hates a brother or sister is a liar. For whoever does not love their brother and sister, whom they have seen, cannot love God, whom they have not seen. (1 John 4:20)

Look at your hand again and think back to those five areas of your life. Just as all areas of your life can work together to serve God, all of those same areas can work together to help others. But if you use only one area—one *finger*—to help someone, you will not accomplish as much as when you use your whole self.

The Needs and Strengths of a Family

God's intention for us is to grow. In John 10:10, Jesus tells us, "I have come that they may have life, and have it to the full." A "full" or *abundant* life has its needs met in all areas and continues to improve in each area.

Our lives might not always seem abundant. Sometimes it is easier to see our problems than our strengths. But if we take a close look at our lives, all of us can find strengths. It is important to name our strengths so we can build on them.

> **We cannot separate loving God from loving our neighbors.**

As you read the following story about Sarah and John, think about this family's needs and their strengths in all the areas of development—their physical, mental, emotional, and social needs and their need for healthy choices.

1. Discuss this family's situation and their *needs* in the areas of development:

- physical
- mental
- social
- emotional
- good choices
- spiritual

SARAH AND HER FAMILY

Sarah, a woman living in a rural village, is married to John. Sarah and John have five children and own their house. The house is small and often filled with children's laughter. Sarah works hard each day in their small plot of land, growing crops to feed her family. She sells the surplus at the market. With the profit she pays for her children's school fees but she can only afford to send the two boys to school.

Sarah came from a family of many children who were often hungry. After she finished third grade she had to stay home to help in the garden and care for the younger children, so Sarah did not learn to read or write. She believes that she is not smart enough to make good decisions so she often seeks advice from others.

Some years ago John was accused of cursing someone from a neighboring village. The men from that family beat him badly, and now he has a bad limp. Sadly, there is still anger between their families. John works as a day laborer, but because he has a weak leg he is always the last one chosen for a job.

In general, Sarah and John get along well with their neighbors, but Sarah thinks that the neighbors may look down on them because they are poor. Sarah is happy that John is a faithful husband who works hard. They always talk about their problems together.

Sarah and John do not attend any church regularly, but whenever Sarah does attend she feels happy and less worried.

Today, Sarah is working in her garden. The sun is very hot, and the ground is hard. She squints to look at clouds on the horizon. *Will it rain?* she wonders. She is very worried that her family will be hungry if the crop does not do well.

2. Now discuss this family's *strengths* in each of those same areas:

- physical
- mental
- social

- emotional
- good choices
- spiritual

God is not only interested in your spiritual growth but also deeply interested in your physical, emotional, and social well-being. He loves you and desires to bless you in all these areas. He has given us all strengths, but we also have needs that hinder us from experiencing the fullness of life he wants us to have. Our development in every area of our lives will enable us to experience more of what God has in store for us.

➤ Review

- What is development?

- What different areas of our lives need to grow and develop for us to be whole and complete?

- What does God ask us to do with each of these areas of our lives?

◇ Reflect

Look back at your hand and consider your own life. Name one strength you have in each area of development:

- physical
- mental
- social

- emotional
- good choices
- spiritual

two

UNDERSTANDING POVERTY

✔ **Objectives**

- Identify some of the characteristics of very poor and vulnerable people in the community.
- Examine what God says about the origin of poverty.
- Explore how broken relationships are part of the cycle of poverty.
- Discover God's plan to rescue people and the world from sin.

Thinking About Poverty

We all have needs and challenges in many areas of our lives. Some people lack enough food and shelter. Others struggle to afford schooling for their children. Many have strained relationships with family members.

Close your eyes and think of someone in your community who lacks the basic resources needed to survive. If you don't know such people, what can you do to get to know them?

1. Describe this person's life.

2. Describe this person's family.

3. What kinds of problems does this person face in the five areas of development discussed in the previous session?

4. What makes this person vulnerable in terms of health, welfare, and relationships?

> **Poverty is more than just a lack of money.**

Poverty affects the physical, mental, emotional, and social development of a person as well as the ability to make good choices. More than just a lack of money, poverty is about unmet needs in all areas of a person's life.

The Origins of Poverty

Why is there poverty in our world? To understand the root causes of poverty, we must go back to the very beginning. God did not create the world with poverty and suffering. His plan was good and for our benefit. Read about God's original plan for humankind and for our relationships in Genesis 1 and 2.

1. What did God say after each day of creation? (Genesis 1:10, 12, 18, 21, 25, 31)

2. How did God create man and woman? (Genesis 1:26-27)

3. How did Adam and Eve relate to each other? (Genesis 2:18-25)

4. What is God's relationship with Adam and Eve? (Genesis 1:28-30)

In the creation account, we recognize three different types of relationships: between people and God, between people, and between people and God's creation. As you think about these relationships, reflect on the five areas of development for Adam and Eve.

5. How did God provide for their different needs?

- physical
- emotional
- social

- mental
- good choices
- spiritual

As we can see, good relationships helped meet all areas of Adam and Eve's needs. Then and now, God wants us to know and love him, to get along well with others, and to care for the world he created.

The Fall and Poverty

Creation is the story of perfect relationships between God and people, people with each other, and people with the world God created. But we know that our world is not like that today.

Sin entered the world when Adam and Eve believed the lies of Satan instead of God's truth and chose to disobey God. Their sin broke their good relationships with God, with each other and with the world God created.

Life was much more difficult after that, and their needs were not met. Because of sin, suffering and poverty entered the world. Read about the fall of humankind in Genesis 3:

> Now the serpent was more crafty than any of the wild animals the LORD God had made. He said to the woman, "Did God really say, 'You must not eat from any tree in the garden'?"

The woman said to the serpent, "We may eat fruit from the trees in the garden, but God did say, 'You must not eat fruit from the tree that is in the middle of the garden, and you must not touch it, or you will die.'"

"You will not certainly die," the serpent said to the woman. "For God knows that when you eat from it your eyes will be opened, and you will be like God, knowing good and evil."

When the woman saw that the fruit of the tree was good for food and pleasing to the eye, and also desirable for gaining wisdom, she took some and ate it. She also gave some to her husband, who was with her, and he ate it. Then the eyes of both of them were opened, and they realized they were naked; so they sewed fig leaves together and made coverings for themselves.

Then the man and his wife heard the sound of the LORD God as he was walking in the garden in the cool of the day, and they hid from the LORD God among the trees of the garden. But the LORD God called to the man, "Where are you?"

He answered, "I heard you in the garden, and I was afraid because I was naked; so I hid."

And he said, "Who told you that you were naked? Have you eaten from the tree that I commanded you not to eat from?"

The man said, "The woman you put here with me—she gave me some fruit from the tree, and I ate it."

Then the LORD God said to the woman, "What is this you have done?"

The woman said, "The serpent deceived me, and I ate."

So the LORD God said to the serpent, "Because you have done this,

"Cursed are you above all livestock
    and all wild animals!
You will crawl on your belly
    and you will eat dust
    all the days of your life.
And I will put enmity
    between you and the woman,
    and between your offspring and hers;
he will crush your head,
    and you will strike his heel."

To the woman he said,

"I will make your pains in childbearing very severe;
    with painful labor you will give birth to children.
Your desire will be for your husband,
    and he will rule over you."

To Adam he said, "Because you listened to your wife and ate fruit from the tree about which I commanded you, 'You must not eat from it,'

"Cursed is the ground because of you;
    through painful toil you will eat food from it
    all the days of your life.
It will produce thorns and thistles for you,
    and you will eat the plants of the field.
By the sweat of your brow
    you will eat your food
until you return to the ground,
    since from it you were taken;
for dust you are
    and to dust you will return." (Genesis 3:1-19)

1. What did the serpent (Satan) tell Eve? (vv. 4-5)

2. Did Eve and Adam believe the lie of Satan? What did they do? (v. 6)

3. How did Adam and Eve respond after eating the fruit? (vv. 7-8)

More than just shame, there were other very real consequences for sin.
4. How did the fall change their lives?

   Eve (v. 16)

   Adam (vv. 17-19)

Adam and Eve were then forced to leave the garden. As time passed, they had two sons. Abel kept herds of animals, and Cain grew crops in the fields. When Abel's sacrifice was accepted by God but Cain's wasn't, Cain became angry and jealous. Read about Cain and Abel in Genesis 4.

5. What did Cain do? (Genesis 4:8)

> **Broken relationships are a major cause of poverty and suffering.**

The story of the fall of humankind teaches us that broken relationships—a broken relationship with God, broken relationships with ourselves, broken relationships with each other, and broken relationships with the world that God created—are a major cause of poverty and suffering. Poverty is not so much about the lack of material things and money as it is about broken relationships.

6. How did sin affect the good relationship between people and God?

7. How did sin affect the good relationship between people?

8. How did sin affect the good relationships between people and the created world around them?

God's plan was for peaceful, strong relationships. Sin broke these good relationships. Broken relationships make life much more difficult and increase poverty in many ways. By understanding how broken relationships cause hardship and poverty, we realize poverty is more than just a lack of material things. Poverty is when we lack in any area of life.

9. What are some examples of how broken relationships—between God and people, between people, and between people and creation—can lead to poverty?

A Very Sad Day for Sarah

As you read this story about Sarah and her family, pay attention to the different types of relationships in the story and all the ways poverty affects this family.

SARAH'S SON

Today was the saddest day of Sarah's life: today her baby died.

Two days ago, her baby son had a high fever and would not stop crying. Sarah was so afraid. On the advice of her grandmother, Sarah took her baby to the healer. She paid him with the money she had saved for school fees, so he performed a ritual for her son and said, "Tomorrow your son will be back to normal."

But the next day, Sarah's son was still burning with fever and very still. Sarah begged a neighbor to loan her money for transport. Unfortunately, she had to wait a long time for the taxi so several hours passed before they reached the health clinic. Soon after she arrived, her baby died.

"You stupid village woman," the nurse shouted. "Your baby died from malaria caused by mosquito bites. Why did you wait so long to come to the clinic? If your baby had treatment sooner, he may not have died."

Tears ran down Sarah's cheeks as she remembered her baby's face. She felt helpless and hopeless and alone. "God, where are you when I need you?" she cried.

1. How did poverty affect Sarah when her baby was sick?

2. What were some of the reasons Sarah did not take her baby to the clinic right away?

3. In what ways is the relationship broken between God and Sarah?

4. How does the story show broken relationships with others?

5. How does this story show a broken relationship between humankind and creation?

God's Rescue Plan for the World

In this story, Sarah felt very helpless and hopeless. But Sarah—and others—are not forgotten by God. After Adam and Eve sinned, God began his great work of bringing people and his broken world back into a loving and healthy relationship with him. As it says in the Bible:

> For God so loved the world that he gave his one and only Son, that whoever believes in him shall not perish but have eternal life. (John 3:16)

1. What can we learn about God from this verse?

That's good news, but that isn't the whole story. After Jesus, God's son, died on the cross, God raised him from the dead on the third day. We could have no hope of eternal life if God had not raised Jesus from the dead. He is alive today and calling us to repent of our sins in order to restore our relationship with God. The Bible reminds us that we can't earn a relationship with God through our own efforts:

> For it is by grace you have been saved, through faith—and this is not from yourselves, it is the gift of God—not by works, so that no one can boast. (Ephesians 2:8-9)

But how do we have a relationship with God?

> If we confess our sins, he is faithful and just and will forgive us our sins and purify us from all unrighteousness. (1 John 1:9)

> Yet to all who did receive him, to those who believed in his name, he gave the right to become children of God. (John 1:12)

> **God wants you to help people know him and know what he has done for them.**

2. What does God promise when we confess our sins and believe in his name?

If you have never confessed your sin and become God's child, maybe today is the day. All you need to do is pray this simple prayer:

> *I confess to God that I am a sinner and believe that the Lord Jesus Christ died for my sins on the cross and was raised for my salvation. I do now receive and confess him as my personal Savior. Amen.*

Now as a Christian, you have the honor to belong to the church that God has set up to do his will in this world. God has given you an important job to do. He wants you to help people know him and know what he has done for them.

He also expects us, with his help, to begin to restore this world into what he intended it to be. As his children we can begin to help the sick, protect our forests, care for the widows and orphans, and do many other things that he is calling us to do.

☞ Review

- In what ways can a person be poor?

- What are some examples of how broken relationships—between God and people, between people, and between people and creation—can lead to poverty?

- How does God's rescue plan restore broken relationships?

◇ Reflect

Because people disobeyed God and turned their backs on him, life became hard and people became poor. But God loves his world and the people in it, so he sent Jesus to die on the cross to rescue us from our sinful ways.

- If you believe in Jesus, thank him for saving you and ask him to show you how you can join in loving and caring for the people around you.

- If you have not yet believed that Jesus died in your place for your sin, speak to a pastor or a church leader. Ask them to show you how to pray for God's forgiveness and become one of his children.

three

GOD'S COMPASSION FOR THE POOR

✔ **Objectives**

- Consider God's compassion for the poor.
- Express why the church should help people in need.
- Describe the characteristics of the most vulnerable in your community.

God's Good Gifts

Losing a child is devastating for any parent. But the nurse's cruel words added unbearable pain to Sarah's grief: she felt responsible for her son's death.

ANNIE

Sarah thought God had abandoned her. She was very sad.

As she sat under a tree shelling beans she was deep in thought. *What could the clinic workers have done to save my son?* she wondered.

That evening Sarah noticed that her four-year-old daughter, Annie, did not eat the food Sarah had prepared for her. The next morning Annie's skin felt hot when Sarah washed and dressed her. She shared her worry with her husband John.

"Another sick child! Is our family cursed?" shouted John. "And we have no money for the healer."

But Sarah remembered what the nurse said to her: her son had died because she did not bring him to the clinic sooner. She borrowed money for transport from her sister, Grace, and took Annie to the clinic without delay.

At the clinic, the same nurse who had scolded Sarah two weeks earlier examined Annie. "It is good that you brought your daughter to the clinic," the nurse said to Sarah. "She has symptoms of malaria but I can give her medicine that will help her." The nurse provided the medicine and instructed Sarah on how to care for Annie at home.

As Sarah walked back home carrying Annie on her back, she felt happy for the first time since her infant son had died. In spite of not having much education, she knew she had done a good thing for Annie.

1. Why was the outcome different for Sarah's daughter, Annie, than for her baby son?

2. What does this story tell us about the ways God helps us and shows us that he loves us?

Medicine that fights malaria is also part of God's rescue plan. He has given people minds with the knowledge to make medicine that saves the lives of many people who would otherwise die from malaria. God wants to alter the negative consequences of sin on his broken creation.

Think about the ways God loves and cares for us:

Every good and perfect gift is from above, coming down from the Father of the heavenly lights, who does not change like shifting shadows. (James 1:17)

Which of you, if your son asks for bread, will give him a stone? Or if he asks for a fish, will give him a snake? If you, then, though you are evil, know how to give good gifts to your children, how much more will your Father in heaven give good gifts to those who ask him! (Matthew 7:9-11)

3. Why should we trust God and believe that he will provide good things for us?

4. Think about it: What other gifts has God given us to deal with the results of sin in our world?

The Suffering of the Poor

God is especially concerned about people who are in need or are vulnerable. Here is another story about Sarah and her husband, John.

THE MONEYLENDER

While Sarah was helping Annie get well, her gardening hoe and spade went missing. She needed these tools to prepare her garden for planting.

John suspected that someone had stolen the tools. Since they had no money saved to purchase new tools, he went to town on his bicycle to visit the moneylender.

The moneylender always had money to loan, but John knew he could be cruel if loans were not repaid on time.

"I need a loan to buy gardening tools," said John. "Without the tools we cannot plant, and then my children will not have food."

John thought that if he explained the problem, the moneylender would show some mercy. But the moneylender only shook his head and said, "What do you have that is worth anything that I can keep until you pay back your loan?"

John owned very little except his bicycle. But because of his lame leg, his bicycle was the only way he could travel the long distance to town in one day.

"What about that bicycle?" asked the moneylender. John was afraid.

"If you want the money you must leave the bicycle," said the moneylender. "Or maybe your children are not that important to you?" John looked away but nodded in agreement.

"Okay, we have a deal," said the moneylender. "I will keep the bicycle until you repay the loan. And, because I am so generous, the interest rate will only be double the loan. But if you don't pay it back on time along with the interest rate, the bicycle will stay with me. Do you understand?"

"Yes," said John, "I understand." John took the money, purchased the tools, and started the journey back to his home. He knew he would not arrive before nightfall.

Why is life so difficult for Sarah and me? he thought as he limped down the road, carrying the spade and hoe on his shoulders. *We work hard, but it doesn't seem to make a difference. Maybe the ancestors are unhappy with us, or maybe someone has put a curse on us.* John felt sad and alone as he walked toward his home in the dark.

1. In this story, what is causing John and Sarah's hardships?

2. What did John believe was the cause of his troubles?

From this story we see that the suffering of the poor is often a result of other people's sin—their hard hearts, corruption, greed, and cruelty toward others. But God shows concern for the poor:

> Whoever oppresses the poor shows contempt for
>   their Maker,
>   but whoever is kind to the needy honors
>   God. (Proverbs 14:31)

When we care for the poor we honor God, but to oppress the poor is to show disrespect for God.

3. What are some examples of how the poor are oppressed in your community?

> **When we care
> for the poor, we
> honor God.**

4. Where have you seen people showing kindness to the needy in your community?

We are all created in the image of God, so every human being carries within them some reflection of God. Because this is true, we should honor and respect every person we meet. God loves each person. Even those who sin are still loved by God and still bear his image.

Caring for the Needs of Others

In the story about John going to the moneylender, we saw how easily needy people can be oppressed by others. But we know that Sarah and John—and other people in need—are not forgotten by God. Throughout the Bible, God shows his concern and love for very poor people. God also instructs his people to help those who are vulnerable and in need—people like John and Sarah.

Jesus said to his disciples, "As the Father has sent me, I am sending you" (John 20:21). As followers of Christ, he is sending us. What does God's Word say about what we are sent to do?

> Is not this the kind of fasting I have chosen:
> to loose the chains of injustice
>   and untie the cords of the yoke,
> to set the oppressed free
>   and break every yoke?
> Is it not to share your food with the hungry
>   and to provide the poor wanderer with shelter—
> when you see the naked, to clothe them,
>   and not to turn away from your own flesh and blood? (Isaiah 58:6-7)

Then the King will say to those on his right, "Come, you who are blessed by my Father; take your inheritance, the kingdom prepared for you since the creation of the world. For I was hungry and you gave me something to eat, I was thirsty and you gave me something to drink, I was a stranger and you invited me in, I needed clothes and you clothed me, I was sick and you looked after me, I was in prison and you came to visit me."

Then the righteous will answer him, "Lord, when did we see you hungry and feed you, or thirsty and give you something to drink? When did we see you a stranger and invite you in, or needing clothes and clothe you? When did we see you sick or in prison and go to visit you?"

The King will reply, "Truly I tell you, whatever you did for one of the least of these brothers and sisters of mine, you did for me." (Matthew 25:34-40)

Suppose a brother or a sister is without clothes and daily food. If one of you says to them, "Go in peace; keep warm and well fed," but does nothing about their physical needs, what good is it? In the same way, faith by itself, if it is not accompanied by action, is dead. (James 2:15-17)

1. How should we respond to the needs of the poor and oppressed?

2. Why should we care for the poor and oppressed?

These passages help us recognize that God is concerned for all of the needs of the poor, not just their physical needs. To care for the poor is to care for Christ.

In the last session we learned that we do not get to heaven by doing good works. Our salvation is a gift from God, so we care for the poor because we are already saved and want to live for Christ. We act out of gratitude.

Who Are the Most Vulnerable?

The Bible teaches us that God cares about poor people. As members of his church, he expects us to help them.

Think back to those areas in which people need to develop. We have needs in all of these areas. But we also know that some in our community have more needs than others. God tells us that we are to help them.

Often we focus on only our material needs when we talk about poverty, but there can be poverty and need in all areas of life and development.

Take Sarah and her husband John as an example: they are poor and have problems in their lives, but Sarah and John have a good relationship. John works as hard as he can for the family and is a faithful husband. Sarah has a sister, Grace, who is also married with children. Grace and her family earn more money than Sarah and John and have a nicer house, but Grace's husband often comes home drunk. He badly beats Grace and the children, shouting curse words at them. Because of this Grace and her children live in fear.

> To care for the poor is to care for Christ.

Compare Sarah and Grace.

1. Who is better off materially?

2. Who is better off relationally?

3. Who is better off emotionally?

As you can see, money isn't everything! Keep this in mind as you fill out the chart below. Think of the characteristics of people who are well-off and flourishing in these areas of development and then characteristics of people who are needy or impoverished in these areas of development.

Table 1

	Characteristics of those who are well-off and flourishing	Characteristics of those who are needy or impoverished
emotional		
mental		
physical		
social		
good choices		
spiritual		

As we think about poverty and the needs of people in *all* areas of development, we need to remember that God calls us to help and serve others—to come alongside them:

> Carry each other's burdens, and in this way you will fulfill the law of Christ. If anyone thinks they are something when they are not, they deceive themselves. Each one should test their own actions. Then they can take pride in themselves alone, without comparing themselves to someone else, for each one should carry their own load. (Galatians 6:2-5)

We obey God by helping people carry their burdens when they are too heavy to carry alone. But it is important to understand the difference between burden and load. Both are used in Galatians 6:2-5. The word translated as "burden" (Greek *baros*) in verse 2 refers to something that is too big for one person to carry. That is why Paul says that we are obligated to "carry each other's burdens." In verse 5 the word that is translated as "load" (Greek *phortion*) refers to something that one person is able to carry—still heavy but manageable, such as the backpack of a soldier. We are each instructed to carry that which we can handle and be responsible for. Doing for others what they can do for themselves is disempowering and against God's clear instructions: "each one should carry their own load." At the same time, not helping those who struggle with problems too big to handle on their own is also wrong. In assisting the poor, one of the greatest challenges is to discern between burdens and loads.

●◆ Review

• What are some of the good gifts that God has given us?

• Thinking back to the verses we read, how does God view poor people?

• How does God view those who oppress the poor?

• What are some things God instructs us to do for the poor?

• What are the characteristics of the most vulnerable poor people in your community?

◇ Reflect

Is there a very poor person you know that you could respectfully ask about their life? If so, ask them to tell you why they think they are poor and how the challenges they face make their life more difficult. Listen to how they understand their own situation. If you do not know someone to have this conversation with, think about how Sarah and John might understand their situation.

four

THE TRANSFORMATION TREE

✔ **Objectives**

- Explore the concept of transformation and the connection of beliefs, values, actions, and behavior.
- Review how God created us as whole and complete people, and relate this to growing and being transformed in all areas of life.

The Transformation Tree

In the first session, we used the illustration of a seed growing into a tree to think about growth and development in our lives and community. Keeping in mind the different areas of development, let's revisit the image of a seed becoming a tree as we explore how our beliefs and values influence our actions and behaviors.

As you look at the tree, notice its four major parts: roots, trunk, branches, and fruit.

1. If this tree were a picture of your life, what part of the tree represents what you believe—what you think is true?

2. What part of the tree represents what you value?

Figure 1. Transformation tree

3. What part of the tree represents your actions and behaviors?

4. What part of the tree represents the results or consequences of your actions and behaviors?

Take a moment and think about the roots of a tree.

5. What happens to a tree if its roots are weak and shallow?

> **Our beliefs shape all aspects of our lives.**

6. What happens to a tree with very strong and healthy roots?

The roots help the rest of the tree—trunk, branches, leaves, and fruit—to grow well. If the roots are healthy, the tree will be healthy.

It is the same way with people. The roots of your tree—your beliefs—determine your values, which in turn direct your actions and decisions, yielding results and consequences—"fruit"—of those actions. Just as the quality of the fruit is determined by the health of the entire tree, the results of our actions are either good or bad depending on what we believe and value.

Good growth starts from the roots of a tree. In the same way, only growth that starts at the roots or the heart of a person based on good beliefs—truth—will lead to a transformed life. Our beliefs, what is believed to be true, shape all aspects of our lives.

A Family Transformed

Sarah and John have neighbors named Elizabeth and Jacob. As you read this story about Elizabeth and Jacob, think about what they believe and value, how their beliefs and values relate to their behaviors or actions, and the results of their actions.

ELIZABETH AND JACOB

Elizabeth and Jacob have four children. They believe all of their children are made in God's image just as Adam and Eve were made in God's image when they were created. So they believe children are a gift from God and entrusted to parents to nurture and protect them as they grow.

With information from the village health workers and staff at the local clinic, Elizabeth and Jacob have learned how to keep their children healthy. They know that good food is important and helps children grow and develop both physically and mentally. Elizabeth breastfed her children and now feeds them fresh fruits and vegetables from her garden and eggs, meat, and fish that she purchases at the market.

Elizabeth and Jacob also know that immunizations protect children from preventable diseases, so all of their children have been immunized. They know the importance of clean water for drinking and cooking, so they provide that for their family. They know how to prevent malaria by removing standing water where mosquitoes multiply and using bed nets when they sleep. They also know the importance of hand washing, especially after using the latrine, and what to do if their children have fever or diarrhea. As a result, their children are strong and healthy and doing well at school.

1. What are the beliefs—the roots—of Elizabeth and Jacob in this story?

2. What are their values—the trunk?

3. In this story, what are Elizabeth's actions—the branches?

4. What are the results that Elizabeth and Jacob see—the fruit?

Bearing Good Fruit

Jesus also used the example of a tree and its fruit to explain how what we believe—what is stored in our hearts—affects the kind of "fruit" or results we can expect in our lives.

> No good tree bears bad fruit, nor does a bad tree bear good fruit. Each tree is recognized by its own fruit. People do not pick figs from thornbushes, or grapes from briers. A good man brings good things out of the good stored up in his heart, and an evil man brings evil things out of the evil stored up in his heart. For the mouth speaks what the heart is full of. (Luke 6:43-45)

1. What is the relationship between the contents of our hearts and what we say and do?

Those who wish to be transformed must first consider their beliefs and values, because what we believe ultimately determines how we live.

Here is a story that will help us think about the difference between changes in appearance and real transformation.

THE SNAKE AND THE CATERPILLAR

One day the snake and the caterpillar were wondering why people disliked them, so they both decided that they needed to change how they looked to others. The snake went away for a while and shed its skin. He returned to where the people lived so they could see him, but when people saw him they took up stones to kill him.

The caterpillar, on the other hand, took the same amount of time and was transformed into a butterfly. When people saw him they were delighted and said to the butterfly, "Come and stay in my garden."

2. What was the difference between what happened to the snake and what happened to the caterpillar?

It is possible for people to make surface changes like the snake, but internally they remain unchanged. Sooner or later, others will realize that they are still the same.

But others, like the butterfly, experience change deep within, and their whole life is affected. When we begin to believe God's truth, it can cause this kind of deep change. It's then that we are truly transformed. The Bible tells us that when we experience that kind of transformation, the evidence is in how we treat others:

But the fruit of the Spirit is love, joy, peace, forbearance, kindness, goodness, faithfulness, gentleness and self-control. (Galatians 5:22-23)

When we begin to believe God's truths and allow his Spirit to work in our hearts and lives, these are the fruits that can appear. This is the evidence of the transforming work of the Spirit.

Just as the tree begins as a seed underneath the ground and then develops deep roots, transformation starts inside of us—in our hearts. When we turn our lives over to God, his Spirit lives in us, and we become his children.

As we study God's Word, the Spirit reveals to us what is good and true, and our beliefs change. Then we begin valuing what God values, and our actions reflect the truth we believe. As a result, we act in ways that honor God and show love to our neighbors. This is the process of transformation.

Growth That Brings Transformation

The best development—the best growth—is the kind
that changes both the way we think *and* the way we act.
God created us as whole people, and he wants us to grow
in all areas of our lives.

Think about the five areas of development.

1. What is it that controls all these areas of your life?

2. As you think about the transformation tree, how does
   God begin to grow and transform you?

> When we allow
> God's truth to be
> the foundation
> for our values
> and actions, we
> can be truly
> transformed.

3. As your beliefs—what you know to be true—begin to
   change, how will that affect the rest of your life?

We are transformed when positive growth begins to
happen in all areas of our lives: physical, emotional,
mental, social, and how we go about making choices.

As we learned in sessions two and three, sin and wrong
beliefs have caused problems in every area of our lives
and our relationships. Our own sin can prevent us from
growing into the people God intended us to be. But the
sins of others also affect all areas of our lives.

Our own brokenness and the brokenness around us
contribute to poverty—poverty in our relationships,
poverty in our thinking, and emotional poverty like

feelings of hopelessness and despair that cause us to make unwise choices. But when we allow God's truth to be the foundation for our values and actions, we can be truly transformed.

The Transformation of Sarah's Neighbor

Transformational development happens in everyday life, gradually changing people's hearts and minds, resulting in new actions and fruits. Development that transforms is something that can happen to each one of us. Here is a story about Elizabeth's transformation.

ELIZABETH

Life was hard for Elizabeth a few years ago. She used all the money she had to feed and clothe her children and never had any left over. Some of the women in Elizabeth's church encouraged her to join a group called a Savings Club. Elizabeth didn't believe she could save money each week as the club required. However, she faithfully attended the meetings and learned useful information about managing the resources she had and how to make more profit.

Every week Elizabeth saved a small amount of money. It was very hard at first but the other women in the group encouraged her. Little by little, the amount of money she saved grew. Elizabeth used her savings to expand her kitchen garden. Then she started selling the extra vegetables and saved a little more each week. She began to see herself in a new way—as a person who could improve her life. She started to realize that God had given her talents and was thankful to him. Through a Bible study after her group meetings, Elizabeth grew in her knowledge and relationship with God.

Because Elizabeth believed God loved her, she grew more confident. Soon, her actions began reflecting this confidence. She attended other lessons about keeping her children healthy, and she also saved money for emergencies. Eventually with her savings and profits she had enough money to send all of her children to school, even her two daughters. Other women admired Elizabeth and would often ask for her advice.

When Elizabeth heard the sad news about the death of her neighbor Sarah's baby, she gathered some vegetables and began preparing a stew to give to Sarah's family. "I will do what I can to help them," said Elizabeth.

1. At first, what were Elizabeth's beliefs?

2. What new beliefs helped change her actions?

3. How did her new beliefs help accomplish good things in her life?

Jesus said that God's greatest commands are that we should "love the Lord with all our heart and all our soul and all our strength and our entire mind" and to "love our neighbor as ourselves."

4. How did Elizabeth's actions and choices show her love for God and others?

◆◆ Review

• How do our beliefs influence the results of our actions?

• What are some of the beliefs about people that can hinder us from loving our neighbors as we love ourselves?

• In the story, Elizabeth began to see herself in a new way. How did that impact her life? How does what you believe about yourself impact your life?

◇ Reflect

How can you show love to a neighbor who needs help? How can believing that God loves you bring positive change and transformation to your life? Consider one action you could take in one of these two areas.

five

DEVELOPMENT AND TRANSFORMATION

✔ Objectives

- Recall the idea of transformation, using the tree as a model.
- Discover how to identify beliefs, values, actions, and results in everyday situations.

Understanding Transformation from Within

Transformational development, or development that transforms us, is a process of growth based on God's truths. Every area of development—physical, mental, emotional, and social needs, and the choices we make each day—can be transformed by the power of God when he is living within us . . . when we are spiritually alive.

The image of the hand helps us recognize that transformation has a holistic affect on our bodies, minds, feelings, relationships, and decisions. The transformation tree embodies the strong relationship between what we believe and value and the resulting actions and outcomes. This model of growth and change can help us understand how God wants us to grow and improve, and how we should help others in need.

Transformational development is deep-down change that can improve every area of life. So when you think about how to grow in a particular area, remember the transformation tree and ask yourself:

What is true? In your heart and mind, you believe that certain things are true. Just as the roots determine how the rest of the tree grows, your beliefs determine your growth.

What is best? Just as the roots are connected to the trunk, your beliefs determine what you value, what is important, what you are willing to make sacrifices for, and how you use your time.

What is done? Your actions are the things you do and the way you behave. As the branches of the tree are a natural extension of the trunk, your behavior and actions are a reflection of your values.

Results and Consequences
What is seen?

Behavior and Actions
What is done?

Values
What is best?

Beliefs
What is true?

Figure 2. Transformation tree

What is seen? These are the results or consequences of the actions and behaviors you choose. Just as the fruit and leaves are evidence of the tree's growth, results and consequences reflect your choices.

Consider a good example of fruit in the area of mental development, such as a child who has completed schooling.

1. What are some of the specific actions that led to this result?

Transformational development is deep-down change that can improve every area of life.

2. What do the child's parents value?

3. What does a person who thinks it is best to educate a child believe about that child's mental development?

Now think of a child who is *not* educated.

4. What are the beliefs that led to this result?

5. What are some of the results if a child does not get an education?

Understanding the Transformation Tree

Use these following short stories to fill out the chart below. As you read, identify the beliefs, values, behaviors or actions, and the results in each story.

Table 2

	Jacob and Elizabeth	Elizabeth	Daniel	Daniel and Agnes
What is seen: Results				
What is done: Behaviors/ Actions				
What is best: Values				
What is true: Beliefs				

JACOB AND ELIZABETH

Sarah's neighbors, Elizabeth and Jacob, have four healthy children. They have been married for fifteen years. Jacob believes that all people—men and women—are equal because they are all created in the image of God. When Elizabeth was pregnant with their first child, Jacob thought it was best for her to receive prenatal care and learn how to take care of herself, so Jacob gave Elizabeth money for transport to the clinic. At the clinic, Elizabeth was encouraged to come with her husband to be tested for HIV in case she needed to take medicine to keep the baby from being infected. Jacob agreed, and they both tested negative. When Elizabeth was ready to deliver, Jacob took her to the maternity clinic. After Elizabeth gave birth to a healthy baby, she and Jacob thanked God for the child.

ELIZABETH

Elizabeth loves her children and believes that they are a gift from God and that they need her help to develop and grow. She values the information she has learned from the health workers about the importance of hygiene, good nutrition, and how to prevent diseases. Because she values this information, she gives her children good food clean water and teaches them good hygiene. She also makes sure they are immunized against preventable diseases and that they receive treatment if they are sick. She has encouraged other women in her family, church, and community to attend the health lessons. Because of this, Elizabeth's children are healthy and there has been less sickness and death among infants from diarrhea and malaria in her community.

DANIEL

Sarah has a cousin named Daniel. They started school the same year. When Sarah had finished the third grade, her parents stopped sending her to school, and she stayed home to help in the garden. Daniel attended school through eighth grade. After leaving school, Daniel learned from some agricultural extension workers about how to keep the soil fertile. Daniel believes that God made the earth and people are protectors of God's creation. Daniel values the land and thinks it is important to take care of it and not just use it up. For example, Daniel practices crop rotation—he switches what crops he plants on his land each season. Because of this, the soil remains fertile and Daniel has very good crops.

DANIEL AND AGNES

Daniel is married to Agnes. Daniel and Agnes believe that having a good house—a good shelter—helps people have a better life. They know that often in their community, when a woman's husband dies, she and her children are forced out by other family members who want the house for themselves. They know this causes great suffering for families, and it troubles them. They believe the Bible when it says that it pleases God to care for widows and orphans: "Religion that God our Father accepts as pure and faultless is this: to look after orphans and widows in their distress" (James 1:27).

Daniel, Agnes, and their church congregation think it is best to protect the rights of widows and orphans by allowing them to stay in their homes even after the man of the house dies. So when the head of a household dies in their community, Daniel and Agnes go with their church group to the local government and ask the officials to protect the inheritance rights of the widow and her children. As a result, the government has begun to take action. Now, widows and children in their community are much more likely to keep their homes and land.

This chart (table 2, p. 51) helps us recognize that beliefs and values shape behaviors, actions, and results. The positive results and outcomes that we see in these stories and in the world around us had their beginning in good beliefs and values.

Now take a look at the areas of development in these stories. Identify actions and results in these stories from the different areas of life:

- physical
- social

- mental
- good choices

- emotional

As we have seen, what we believe and value determines the results and consequences of our actions and behavior. Good actions and good results can help people around us, especially people who are the most vulnerable and in the greatest need.

Bearing Good Fruit

One time when Jesus taught about development and growth, instead of a tree he used the image of a grapevine:

> I am the vine; you are the branches. If you remain in me and I in you, you will bear much fruit; apart from me you can do nothing. If you do not remain in me, you are like a branch that is thrown away and withers; such branches are picked up, thrown into the fire and burned. If you remain in me and my words remain in you, ask whatever you wish, and it will be done for you. This is to my Father's glory, that you bear much fruit, showing yourselves to be my disciples. (John 15:5-8)

To *remain* or *abide* in Jesus means that we follow him closely and know him well because we know his Word. But this invitation is more than simply following him— this is an invitation to have a relationship with him: to know him *and* to be known by him. Remarkable!

> **Good actions and good results can help people who are the most vulnerable and in the greatest need.**

1. What does this passage tell us about how we bear fruit?

2. When we bear fruit, what does that reveal to others around us?

3. What are some ways you "remain" in Jesus? What do you do to stay connected to him and follow him?

Jesus also used the image of a tree to teach about fruit being the evidence of our connection to him:

> No good tree bears bad fruit, nor does a bad tree bear good fruit. Each tree is recognized by its own fruit. (Luke 6:43-44)

4. When you remain in Jesus, what kinds of fruit do you think you can expect to see?

To be a disciple of Jesus is to follow him, and when we follow him our minds are renewed and our lives are transformed:

> Do not conform to the pattern of this world, but be transformed by the renewing of your mind. Then you will be able to test and approve what God's will is—his good, pleasing and perfect will. (Romans 12:2)

Here we learn that we are transformed when our minds are renewed. A renewed mind is one that knows how to follow God because it recognizes "his good, pleasing and perfect will." In other words, a renewed mind is a mind that believes in God's truth.

5. How can having a renewed mind transform you?

So the Bible is talking about growth in every area of life. That growth, or "fruit," is evidence of God working in and through us. And when we are attached to Jesus—when we know him well and follow him closely—our fruit begins to resemble his fruit. Jesus' fruit was helping people

- come to know him as the giver of eternal life;
- overcome obstacles in their lives that kept them in bondage to unhealthy life decisions;
- see that they had worth and value in the eyes of God; and
- realize that there would be difficulties in this life, but that he would provide strength, guidance, and peace as they stayed connected to him.

When we are connected to God—when we believe his truth, know his Word, and follow him—our minds are renewed, and we begin to see all of life differently.

●◆ Review

- What is the connection of beliefs, values, actions, and results?

- What produces good results, or good fruit, in our lives?

- What must we believe in order for our minds to be renewed?

◇ Reflect

Think about how you will use the model of the transformation tree to tell one person in your church or community about what you are learning. Prepare to explain— either by writing it out or practicing on a friend—how beliefs and values lead to actions, and actions lead to results.

six

HARMFUL BELIEFS AND POVERTY

✔ Objectives
- Identify harmful beliefs that lead to poverty.
- Consider poverty in all areas of development.
- Recognize that transformational development means aligning our beliefs with God's truth.

A Strong Marriage

As you read the following story about Jacob and Elizabeth, think about what they *believe*, what they *value*, what *actions* they take, and the *results* of those actions.

JACOB AND ELIZABETH

When Jacob and Elizabeth were married, they promised to be faithful to each other. They believe marriage and sex within marriage is a very special relationship, ordained by God, and they value being faithful and following God's commands.

Jacob is a trader, and when he travels to other towns he is tempted to have sex with other women, but he resists and stays faithful because he loves Elizabeth and believes that God expects him to keep his vow to her. Elizabeth has always been faithful to Jacob and has only had sexual relations with her husband. Because of this, they do not have sexually transmitted diseases such as HIV/AIDS.

As a result, they have a happy and strong marriage.

1. What do Elizabeth and Jacob believe that helps them stay faithful in marriage?

2. What do Elizabeth and Jacob value or think is important for their lives?

3. What do Elizabeth and Jacob do because of what they believe and value?

4. What are the results of their actions?

In Elizabeth and Jacob's story we see how their marriage has been transformed because they believe God's truth about marriage.

Poverty and the Transformation Tree

Use the images of the three trees to answer the questions below.

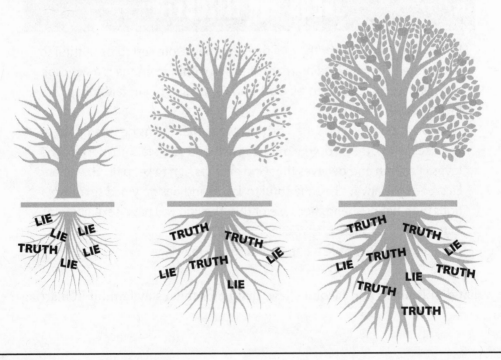

Figure 3. How true beliefs affect growth

1. What differences do you notice in the soil and in the trees?

2. What is the relationship of truth to growth?

3. In place of trees, imagine churches or communities. How is a community affected by the belief of lies?

Jesus illustrated the importance of roots and soil when he told the following parable:

A farmer went out to sow his seed. As he was scattering the seed, some fell along the path, and the birds came and ate it up. Some fell on rocky places, where it did not have much soil. It sprang up quickly, because the soil was shallow. But when the sun came up, the plants were scorched, and they withered because they had no root. Other seed fell among thorns, which grew up and choked the plants. Still other seed fell on good soil, where it produced a crop—a hundred, sixty or thirty times what was sown. (Matthew 13:3-8)

Now imagine individuals in the place of trees as you read how Jesus explained this parable:

When anyone hears the message about the kingdom and does not understand it, the evil one comes and snatches away what was sown in their heart. This is the seed sown along the path. The seed falling on rocky ground refers to someone who hears the word and at once receives it with joy. But since they have no root, they last only a short time. When trouble or persecution comes because of the word, they quickly fall away. The seed falling among the thorns refers to someone who hears the word, but the worries of this life and the deceitfulness of wealth choke the word, making it unfruitful. But the seed falling on good soil refers to someone who hears the word and understands it. This is the one who produces a crop, yielding a hundred, sixty or thirty times what was sown. (Matthew 13:19-23)

Jesus reminds us of the power of lies as well as the power of truth. Our growth and fruitfulness are determined by our beliefs.

Satan, the Father of Lies

The Bible has much to say about Satan and his destructive plans:

> [Satan] was a murderer from the beginning, not holding to the truth, for there is no truth in him. When he lies, he speaks his native language, for he is a liar and the father of lies. (John 8:44)

> The god of this age [Satan] has blinded the minds of unbelievers, so that they cannot see the light of the gospel that displays the glory of Christ, who is the image of God. (2 Corinthians 4:4)

1. What does the Bible say about Satan and his influence?

Think back to session two when we read about Adam and Eve in the Garden of Eden.

2. What did Satan, in the form of a snake, tell Eve? (Genesis 3:4-5)

> **Satan is a liar and a deceiver who wants to lead people away from God's truth and prevent them from having an abundant life.**

Satan is a liar and a deceiver who wants to lead people away from God's truth and prevent them from having an abundant life. If we believe lies instead of God's truth, as Eve did, our actions will bear bitter fruit in our lives. Those lies contribute to poverty in all areas of life—physical, mental, social, emotional, and our ability to make good choices.

Lies That Lead to Bitter Fruit

Poverty is caused by many elements that we cannot control, but what we believe—what is in our hearts and minds—also contributes to the problem. And we can have control over our beliefs. Here are three examples of how false beliefs affect different areas of development and result in bitter fruit.

Mental Development. One reality is that many women and girls have not had the same amount of education as boys and men. Using the lesson of the transformation tree, consider what led to this bitter fruit.

1. What are the results when a girl does not receive an education? What are the fruits?

2. What was done by her parents? What actions did they take?

3. What are the parents' values? What did they think is best or important?

Most parents in the world have a limited amount of money to pay for the schooling of their children. In those situations, oftentimes parents spend money on the education of their sons but not their daughters.

4. What do parents believe about their daughter when they choose not to help her get an education?

5. If an entire country believes this lie, how will the country develop?

Physical and Social Development. There is the false belief, prevalent in the Global South, that having sex with a virgin cures HIV.

6. If a man believes that having sex with a virgin will cure his HIV, what are his values?

7. If he values his life more than the little girl, what actions will he take?

8. If HIV-positive men are having sex with very young girls, what will be the result? What are the outcomes?

Since having sex does not cure HIV, not only do these infected men remain infected, but the consequences of their selfish actions are vast: they infect young girls with HIV, these girls may become pregnant and pass the virus on to their babies, and these girls suffer physically and emotionally, feeling used and discarded. These are some of the bitter fruits that come from believing the harmful lie that having sex with a virgin cures HIV/AIDS.

Making Choices. Consider one more example of a negative outcome or bitter fruit: a man who has no money saved to help his family in times of need. He spends any extra money on alcohol or roasted meat rather than saving it for the future.

9. What are some bitter fruits that can come from not having any money saved?

10. What are some of his actions that led to a lack of savings?

11. What are some of his values that led to these behaviors?

12. What are some beliefs that led him to spend his money this way?

Now think of your own neighborhood and community. Do you recognize evidence of a harmful belief?

13. What are the values of people who hold this belief?

14. What actions are taken because of these values?

15. What are the results and consequences of these actions?

Poverty: The Fruit of Harmful Lies

Beliefs, whether good or bad, shape what we value and what we do in our families and communities every day. As Christians we must earnestly seek God's truth from the Bible. We must also pray for wisdom to identify the harmful lies and speak out against them so others recognize harmful beliefs and the terrible consequences they bring.

As we faithfully teach God's truth and pray for his help, his power will be at work within us:

> Now to him who is able to do immeasurably more than all we ask or imagine, according to his power that is at work within us, to him be glory in the church and in Christ Jesus throughout all generations, for ever and ever! Amen. (Ephesians 3:20-21)

> You, dear children, are from God and have overcome them [false spirits], because the one who is in you is greater than the one who is in the world [Satan]. (1 John 4:4)

Think about it: God is able to do *immeasurably more* than we can even imagine because he is *greater* than the one in the world. God's truth and power are able to withstand and silence all of Satan's lies. To God be the glory!

> **Beliefs, whether good or bad, shape what we value and what we do in our families and communities every day.**

●◆ Review

- What are some of the harmful beliefs that lead to poverty? (Consider how poverty can affect *all* areas of development.)

- How do we overcome Satan's harmful lies that many people believe?

- Where do we get the power to stand against Satan's deception?

◇ Reflect

Consider how easy it is to believe a lie. Make a list of times when believing a lie led to bitter fruit in some area of your life.

seven

REPLACING HARMFUL BELIEFS WITH GOD'S TRUTH

✔ Objectives

- Identify some harmful beliefs that lead to poverty.
- Recognize God's truths that counter these harmful beliefs.
- Consider the role of the church in replacing harmful beliefs with God's truth.

Traditional Beliefs

In your culture, you have many traditions and beliefs that have been taught by parents, grandparents, and others in the community. Some of these beliefs are helpful, but other beliefs are harmful and can increase challenges and cause much suffering.

Consider the following belief: "Cold air causes illness."

1. What are the values that underlie this belief?

2. What actions are taken because of this belief and values?

3. What is the result?

Here is another traditional belief: "Talking to your children about sex will encourage sexual activity at an early age."

4. What are the values of parents who subscribe to this belief?

5. What actions will these parents take?

6. What are the results if parents do not talk to their children about sex?

How Some Traditional Beliefs Lead to Poverty

Read these four stories about Sarah and her family to identify how beliefs and values lead to actions that may cause poverty and suffering. Use these stories to complete the chart.

Table 3

Story	Beliefs	Values	Behavior (Actions)	Results (Consequences)
Grace's beliefs about diet during pregnancy				
Sarah and John's beliefs about curses				
Beliefs about ancestors				
Beliefs about HIV and AIDS				

GRACE'S BELIEFS

Sarah's sister Grace believes the traditional advice given to pregnant women. For example, when she became pregnant, her grandmother firmly told her that pregnant women should not eat meat, so Grace did not eat any meat during her entire pregnancy. But without this important food, Grace became malnourished and weak. As a result, when the baby was born, it was very weak and small.

BELIEFS ABOUT CURSES

Sarah and John are very sad after the death of their baby. They believe someone cursed them and become suspicious of their neighbors. They think, *Is this person angry with us? Maybe he put a curse on us?* As a result, Sarah and John speak less with their neighbors. When they do talk to them, they often argue. When there is a community clean-up day, Sarah and John refuse to cooperate with their neighbors even though a cleaner neighborhood would also benefit their family.

BELIEFS ABOUT ANCESTORS

Sarah is happy when she attends church and says she believes in God and his Word. But since the time she was a young girl she was taught to respect the ancestors, the spirit world, and the witch doctor. Whenever she has a problem—when her crop is failing, when a child is sick—Sarah first turns to the witch doctor for help. It costs her a lot of money each year. People tell Sarah that instead she should spend money on fertilizer for her crops or visits to the clinic, but Sarah isn't sure that spending money on these things instead of the witch doctor will help. She doesn't feel able to make the decision to live in a new way.

BELIEFS ABOUT HIV/AIDS

John, Sarah's husband, has heard a lot of information about HIV from clinics, but deep in his heart he believes that HIV/AIDS is caused by a curse. Because of this, John will not enter a shop owned by a woman named Martha because he heard she has HIV. John will not buy food from Martha's store and tells other people not to go to that store. As a result, Martha has fewer and fewer customers. She earns little money and eventually loses the store. Martha becomes very poor because John and people like him will not purchase goods from her.

1. Some of us may have been raised with these or other traditional beliefs. Who taught you these traditional beliefs?

2. Even though it can be difficult, why is it important to examine *all* of our beliefs—including our traditional ones?

> **We need to examine our beliefs and values to see which ones lead to positive change and which ones keep us in poverty.**

Harmful, false beliefs can damage individuals and entire communities. Some of these long-standing beliefs prevent families and communities from ever changing for the better.

We might see changes in communities only to be disappointed when these changes don't last very long. People sometimes make changes because they are asked or forced to make them, but if their beliefs and values aren't also changed, a community will simply revert back to the old way of doing things.

We recognize the connection between what people believe and poverty, so we need to examine our beliefs and values to see which ones lead to positive change and which ones keep us in poverty.

The Role of the Church

The church has an important role in addressing harmful traditional beliefs in our communities. The church is the only institution that can help people transform their lives—to change in every way and grow in their relationship with God.

The church must help people turn toward beliefs rooted in God's truth.

It can be difficult to let go of beliefs that we have held on to for a long time. From the time we were young, people may have said we need to do these things to protect ourselves and our families. But God—the Almighty God—promises to be our one and only protector.

> Who shall separate us from the love of Christ? Shall trouble or hardship or persecution or famine or nakedness or danger or sword? As it is written:
>
> > "For your sake we face death all day long;
> > we are considered as sheep to be slaughtered."
>
> No, in all these things we are more than conquerors through him who loved us. For I am convinced that neither death nor life, neither angels nor demons, neither the present nor the future, nor any powers, neither height nor depth, nor anything else in all creation, will be able to separate us from the love of God that is in Christ Jesus our Lord. (Romans 8:35-39)

1. What does this passage tell us about the problems that we will face?

2. How might this encourage us to serve Christ alone?

Some beliefs and values lead to bad outcomes—to suffering and poverty in our lives. As Christians, what are we called to do?

> Do not conform to the pattern of this world, but be transformed by the renewing of your mind. Then you will be able to test and approve what God's will is—his good, pleasing and perfect will. (Romans 12:2)

3. According to this verse, what are we Christians to do with our minds?

4. What do you think it means for our minds to be renewed?

5. What is the result of the renewing of our minds?

Remember: God promises to be with us as our minds are renewed. Nothing can separate us from his love.

Transformation in Communities

Think about the consequences of poverty—for example, mothers dying in childbirth.

What actions led to this result? Women might be unwilling to go to the health clinic because it is inconvenient and prefer to give birth at home, they might not have money for the clinic, or their husbands do not want to spend the money for the clinic or for transport.

What do these women value? Women might value their time and familiarity. The men might value money more than their wives' health.

What beliefs produced these values? Women may believe that health clinics are not a good place to give birth. Men may believe women are not as important as they are and don't need or deserve special help during pregnancy and childbirth.

1. What is God's truth that must replace the belief that women are not important and don't deserve special help during pregnancy and childbirth?

> **Nothing can separate us from God's love.**

Now think of a negative fruit of poverty in *your* community. Fill in the elements for the transformation tree below.

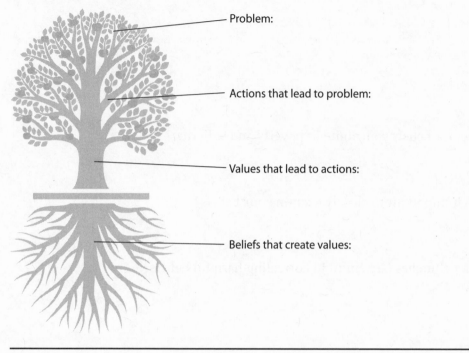

Problem:

Actions that lead to problem:

Values that lead to actions:

Beliefs that create values:

Figure 4.

2. Name one of God's truths that should replace this harmful lie.

Christians in the church need to replace these harmful beliefs with God's truth by knowing and teaching his Word. We can be assured that God will help us and be with us when we teach people about his truths and warn them of the dangers of harmful beliefs. Here we are reminded of the apostle John's teaching:

> You, dear children, are from God and have overcome them [false spirits], because the one who is in you is greater than the one who is in the world. They are from the world and therefore speak from the viewpoint of the world, and the world listens to them. We are from God, and whoever knows God listens to us; but whoever is not from God does not listen to us. This is how we recognize the Spirit of truth and the spirit of falsehood. (1 John 4:4-6)

3. List the truths from this passage of Scripture that can help you counter the harmful beliefs in your community.

⦿ Review

- How do our beliefs contribute to poverty and suffering?

- Why is it important to closely examine our beliefs?

- How can churches be helpful in correcting harmful beliefs?

◈ Reflect

Think about a harmful belief that you know is common in your family or community. Ask God to reveal to you his truth that confronts this harmful belief. Then think about how to start a conversation with someone who needs to believe God's truth rather than Satan's harmful lie.

eight

RELATIONSHIPS AND TRANSFORMATION

✔ Objectives

- Discover God's truth in Jesus' story of the good Samaritan.
- Recognize how healing relationships contribute to improving the lives of the vulnerable.
- Identify practical ways to demonstrate love toward our neighbors.

Healing Relationships

Transformation can happen in all areas of our lives. In session two we discovered that sin affects our relationships. Broken relationships make people vulnerable to many other problems.

1. How do broken relationships between people make them more vulnerable to problems?

2. How does a broken relationship with the created world make people more vulnerable to problems?

3. How does a broken relationship with God make people more vulnerable to problems?

God wants to heal our relationships because healed relationships are an important element of transformed lives. If we ignore broken relationships between God, people, and creation, we cannot bring about true and lasting change. Helping the vulnerable and needy among us requires repairing broken relationships.

Loving God and Loving Our Neighbors

When an expert in the law asked Jesus what he needed to do to inherit eternal life, Jesus said, "Love the Lord" and "love your neighbor" (Luke 10:27). But the expert in the law had a follow-up question for Jesus. He asked, "And who is my neighbor?" To answer, Jesus told a story:

> "A man was going down from Jerusalem to Jericho, when he was attacked by robbers. They stripped him of his clothes, beat him and went away, leaving him half dead. A priest happened to be going down the same road, and when he saw the man, he passed by on the other side. So too, a Levite, when he came to the place and saw him, passed by on the other side. But a Samaritan, as he traveled, came where the man was; and when he saw him, he took pity on him. He went to him and bandaged his wounds, pouring on oil and wine. Then he put the man on his own donkey, brought him to an inn and took care of him. The next day he took out two denarii and gave them to the innkeeper. 'Look after him,' he said, 'and when I return, I will reimburse you for any extra expense you may have.'
>
> "Which of these three do you think was a neighbor to the man who fell into the hands of robbers?"
>
> The expert in the law replied, "The one who had mercy on him." (Luke 10:30-37)

After he was attacked by robbers, this man was naked and half dead, lying in the road. The priest and Levite both saw the man, but refused to stop and help. We all know people who are vulnerable and in need of our help. It is easy for us to "pass by" and not give people the help they need.

> **Helping the vulnerable and needy among us requires repairing broken relationships.**

1. What are some reasons that we don't help others?

The Samaritan is the example of how to be a neighbor because he showed mercy in his care of the robbed and beaten man. Essentially, Jesus says we become "neighbors" when we extend mercy to one another. This is how to love our neighbors.

2. Who are your neighbors?

3. What are some ways you can show mercy to your neighbors?

There's an interesting twist in Jesus' story, because Samaritans were hated and despised by the Jews in those days. The Samaritan was the enemy, but Jesus makes him the role model in the story and reveals that loving our neighbors means loving those who are suspicious of us or even hate us. Jesus expects us to help anyone who is in need, regardless of position, education, religion, wealth, or tribal group. He invites us to be like the Samaritan.

4. Think of people in your family or community that you dislike or distrust. What are ways you can show mercy to them?

> **Jesus expects us to help anyone who is in need, regardless of position, education, religion, wealth, or tribal group. He invites us to be like the Samaritan.**

The man attacked by robbers was robbed of his clothes, beaten, and deprived of his ability to take care of himself. He was *physically* robbed and deprived, but all areas of life are vulnerable to attack.

5. Think of some examples of how we can be robbed or deprived

- physically: • socially:

- mentally: • of our ability to make good choices:

- emotionally: • spiritually:

The man who was attacked by robbers was also found naked. He was physically naked because the robbers had stripped him of his clothes. But people are naked or exposed in other ways—ways that make them feel shame or loss of face. They feel humiliated.

6. What are some ways that people in your community experience shame?

There was a time when nakedness was not a thing of shame.

When God created Adam and Eve, they "were both naked, and they felt no shame" (Genesis 2:25). But sin brought shame and humiliation.

In an act of mercy, God did something wonderful: "The LORD God made garments of skin for Adam and his wife and clothed them" (Genesis 3:21). God gave Adam and Eve a covering for their shame. Even though their shame and vulnerability was the result of their own sin, God still had mercy on them. This act of mercy is an example for God's church.

Think of someone in your family or community who is feeling shame or humiliation. Keep in mind that often problems may not be a direct result of a person's own sin but are a result of sin and trouble in the world.

7. What could you do to show love and mercy to that person? How could you help "cover" that person's shame?

The story of the good Samaritan offers a picture of what it means to be a Christian—to love God and to love your neighbor completely, without holding back. Think back to Jesus' teaching recorded in Matthew 25: "Truly I tell you, whatever you did for one of the least of these brothers and sisters of mine, you did for me" (Matthew 25:40). If we truly love God, we will love our neighbors, because loving our neighbors *is* loving God.

And here we are reminded of the exhortation found in Galatians 6:2: "Carry each other's burdens." Carrying each other's burdens is a wonderful way to show love for one another and for God.

8. What are some examples of ways we can carry each other's burdens?

Another way to love our neighbors is to tell them of God's great love for them and that Jesus Christ died for their sins, rose again, lives today, and wants to be their Savior. The sacrifice of Jesus covers their shame from sin.

> **If we truly love God, we will love our neighbors.**

Compassionate Neighbors

Before you read the stories about Sarah and John, answer the following questions:

1. What has made life difficult for Sarah and John and their family?

2. How have harmful beliefs and broken relationships made them more vulnerable?

3. How are Sarah and John different from their neighbors Elizabeth and Jacob?

ELIZABETH AND SARAH

One afternoon during the heat of the day, Elizabeth visited Sarah. The two sat in the shade of a large mango tree not far from Sarah's gardens. Elizabeth could see that Sarah was feeling sad about the death of her infant son. Elizabeth felt compassion for Sarah. "Sarah, I am sorry that your baby passed away. As a mother myself, I can imagine how difficult it is for you."

Elizabeth told Sarah about attending the health classes and joining the savings club. "I have learned so many useful things," said Elizabeth. "Before, I felt helpless when my children were sick. I wasn't sure how best to help them. But now I know that I can do things to treat their sickness and keep them healthy."

Sarah was very interested in what Elizabeth was sharing. "Tell me more," said Sarah.

"The best part of it," said Elizabeth, "is that it has helped me believe and trust in God in a new way. I'm not afraid of curses against my children. I've learned that God can destroy the power of a curse. And I know that God has given each of us a mind to learn good things that will help us have better lives."

Elizabeth invited Sarah to join the health group, and Sarah agreed to come to the next meeting.

4. How did Elizabeth show love to Sarah?

JACOB AND JOHN

A few days later, Elizabeth's husband, Jacob, visited Sarah's husband, John. Jacob is a trader and was encouraged by his pastor to attend trainings to gain more business skills. Later, Jacob became an elder in the church. Jacob has encouraged men in his church and community to improve their livelihoods using sound business principles; he has also helped them improve their relationships with their wives and communicate better with their children.

When John saw Jacob walking toward his place, he was suspicious. *Why is Jacob here?* John thought. *We don't know each other very well. What does he want from me?*

There was another reason John was suspicious: Jacob is an elder of the local church. *He is probably going to tell me I am bad since I am not attending church,* John thought to himself.

But Jacob showed great respect to John. He asked John about his family, and John felt at ease. After some time Jacob said, "John, you have suffered a great loss with the death of your child. I know when my brother died of an illness, I was angry all the time. I was looking for someone to blame. Sometimes all I wanted to do was go to the bar and get drunk."

Hearing Jacob's story and his honesty helped John feel that Jacob understood what he was going through.

Jacob continued, "What helped me was the encouragement of other people, especially members of my church. They invited me to do things with them so I would spend my time in a good way. They checked in with me regularly and helped me get through a difficult time. It made a big difference, and after some time I began to feel positive about life again."

Jacob told John about the business training that was available and invited John to attend.

"I don't think I could attend," said John. John was ashamed because of his lack of education.

Jacob sensed John's lack of confidence. "My group has people with all different backgrounds—some have had only a little schooling."

John was still unsure, but he appreciated Jacob's kindness and felt it was sincere.

5. How did Jacob show love for his neighbor John?

When people are vulnerable and lack needed resources, their beliefs about themselves and feelings of shame can affect their relationships. But when God transforms people, their beliefs and relationships are restored. They can connect with God, with creation, and with one another in new and positive ways.

> When people are vulnerable and lack needed resources, their beliefs about themselves and feelings of shame can affect their relationships.

The Reconciling Power of Love

Jesus came to reconcile people to God and to one another. Jesus showed no favoritism: he valued everyone equally and gladly shared meals with sinners. So he offered this instruction:

> A new command I give you: Love one another. As I have loved you, so you must love one another. By this everyone will know that you are my disciples, if you love one another. (John 13:34-35)

If we believe that God loves us and that all people are created in his image, we will value every person and act lovingly toward all. When people see our care and compassion for one another—even for our enemies—they will know that we follow God.

God's Word offers us very practical instructions for how to treat others. This passage instructs us in how to restore and keep good relationships:

> Love must be sincere. Hate what is evil; cling to what is good. Be devoted to one another in love. Honor one another above yourselves. Never be lacking in zeal, but keep your spiritual fervor, serving the Lord. Be joyful in hope, patient in affliction, faithful in prayer. Share with the Lord's people who are in need. Practice hospitality.
>
> Bless those who persecute you; bless and do not curse. Rejoice with those who rejoice; mourn with those who mourn. Live in harmony with one another. Do not be proud, but be willing to associate with people of low position. Do not be conceited.
>
> Do not repay anyone evil for evil. Be careful to do what is right in the eyes of everyone. If it is possible, as far as it depends on you, live at peace with everyone. (Romans 12:9-18)

1. List the ways that we can build up our relationships.

2. How does God want us to respond to those who mistreat us?

3. How does God want us to relate and respond to people in need?

When our minds are renewed and our lives are transformed, then our lives are marked by a healthy sense of self and healthy relationships with God and others.

✦ Review

• According to the story of the good Samaritan, who are your neighbors?

• How can healing relationships between people contribute to reducing poverty and improving the lives of the poor?

• What are some practical ways that you can show love to your neighbors?

◇ Reflect

Think about a time when another person encouraged you and reached out when you were going through a difficult time. What did they do that helped?

Now think of a person in your community who is vulnerable or struggling because of circumstances. What one thing could you do to help? Commit to reaching out and showing love to that person.

nine

THE CHURCH AND POVERTY

✔ Objectives

- Identify resources of local churches and link them to needs in the community.
- Identify resources of community members and those outside the community.
- Define the role of the pastor and the congregation in ministry to the poor and vulnerable.

Community Mapping

In the space below, draw a simple map of your community or a neighboring community with its major landmarks. Or if you have recently visited another region, create a map of that community.

- Add the resources that might help the poor and vulnerable: schools, health care facilities, water points, churches, and so on.
- Identify the factors that contribute to poverty in your community: garbage dumps, unclean rivers, and so on.
- Identify where the poor and most vulnerable live.

How Can Churches and Communities Help the Poor?

One reason most people respect the churches in their communities is that those churches do many things to serve their communities.

Think about the different ways churches help people who are poor and in need. Churches doing small things with few resources are just as important as churches doing big projects. Additionally, many different resources—more than just money—exist in each congregation.

1. What are churches in your community already doing to help the poor and vulnerable?

2. In the space below list some of the resources of your church—the skills and strengths of individuals in your congregation.

3. Next to each resource, list one way it could be used to solve a problem in your community. (Refer to your map to remind you of the local problems.)

Problem solving often requires some creative thinking. Keep in mind the transformation tree and the different areas of development as you think of how to put these resources to use.

Now think of people in your community who may not attend a church but who have skills and strengths that could also be used to tackle some of the problems facing your community.

4. List the resources of others in your community. What is it that they do well?

5. How could these resources be used to solve problems in your community?

All Our Skills Come from God

Look over both lists of resources within your church and community. God's Word tells us that it's no coincidence that people have such skills and strengths:

When a farmer plows for planting, does he plow continually?
    Does he keep on breaking up and working the soil?
When he has leveled the surface,
    does he not sow caraway and scatter cumin?
Does he not plant wheat in its place,
    barley in its plot,
    and spelt in its field?
His God instructs him
    and teaches him the right way.

Caraway is not threshed with a sledge,
    nor is the wheel of a cart rolled over cumin;
caraway is beaten out with a rod,
    and cumin with a stick.
Grain must be ground to make bread;
    so one does not go on threshing it forever.
The wheels of a threshing cart may be rolled over it,
    but one does not use horses to grind grain.
All this also comes from the LORD Almighty,
    whose plan is wonderful,
    whose wisdom is magnificent. (Isaiah 28:24-29)

1. What does God say about how the farmer gets his farming knowledge and skill?

2. What does this reveal about God's love and concern for us?

3. How did the people in your church and community get their knowledge, strength, and skills?

Everyone receives his or her knowledge and skills from God. Those who do not have faith in God may not acknowledge him or give thanks to him, but the Bible says their knowledge, skills, and wisdom are still a gift from him.

> Whatever is good and perfect is a gift coming down to us from God our Father. (James 1:17 NLT)

God is gracious: he gives gifts to all of us even though we don't deserve them. Our skills, strength, and knowledge that can be helpful to others and diminish the terrible results of sin in the world are a gift from God Almighty. He wants us to use these skills to do his kingdom work in our communities. God deserves our gratitude and praise for every good gift he has given us.

When we say the Lord's Prayer we pray,

> your kingdom come,
> your will be done,
>   on earth as it is in heaven. (Matthew 6:10)

The church is God's instrument to do his will on earth as it is in heaven. We have magnificent work to do!

Resources Outside the Community

Some problems in our communities cannot be solved by the church alone.

1. List some resources outside your community that could help the poor.

> **God deserves our gratitude and praise for every good gift he has given us.**

2. Is there a problem facing your community that could be solved through the partnership of the church with an outside resource?

Whenever we take action to solve difficult problems in their communities, whether by working alone as the church or with institutions such as the government, NGOs or other groups, we are caring for the poor. And when we care for the poor, we are following God:

> And if you spend yourselves in behalf of the hungry
>> and satisfy the needs of the oppressed,
> then your light will rise in the darkness,
>> and your night will become like the noonday.
> The LORD will guide you always;
>> he will satisfy your needs in a sun-scorched land
>> and will strengthen your frame.
> You will be like a well-watered garden,
>> like a spring whose waters never fail.
>> (Isaiah 58:10-11)

The church is God's presence in the world. God has chosen the church to be his hands and feet: to provide comfort, healing and help to those who are sick, in pain and in need. By loving our neighbors, we express our love for God.

Jesus, Faith, and Works

As Christians, Jesus is our example. But what was his purpose during his time on earth? As he began his teaching ministry, he read this passage in the synagogue:

> The Spirit of the Lord is on me,
>> because he has anointed me
>> to proclaim good news to the poor.
> He has sent me to proclaim freedom for the
>> prisoners

> **The church is God's presence in the world.**

    and recovery of sight for the blind,
        to set the oppressed free,
            to proclaim the year of the Lord's favor. (Luke 4:18-19)

1. What was the purpose of Jesus' ministry?

2. As you think about Jesus' ministry, what did Jesus do aside from preaching and
   teaching?

3. As you look at your community map, do any problems exist in your community
   that Jesus addressed during his life on earth?

   The good news is that all can be reconciled to God. During his time on earth, Jesus
shared this good news by taking care of the sick, the hungry, and the needy. We are
to follow his example and engage in our communities:

   You are the salt of the earth. But if the salt loses its saltiness, how can it be made salty
   again? It is no longer good for anything, except to be thrown out and trampled underfoot.
       You are the light of the world. A town built on a hill cannot be hidden. (Matthew
   5:13-14)

4. How can the church be salt and light to the world?

The local church must have a positive influence on the community. People in the local church must be prepared to go out to the community, listen to their neighbors, find out what their neighbors need, and work together to design programs that meet those needs.

Think back to the transformation tree. Our beliefs are very important because they are the roots that ultimately produce our actions, and our actions are evidence of our beliefs:

> What good is it, my brothers and sisters, if someone claims to have faith but has no deeds? Can such faith save them? Suppose a brother or a sister is without clothes and daily food. If one of you says to them, "Go in peace; keep warm and well fed," but does nothing about their physical needs, what good is it? In the same way, faith by itself, if it is not accompanied by action, is dead. (James 2:14-17)

5. According to this passage, what does a person with living faith look like?

6. When do we show that we truly believe in and love God?

Our Roles in the Church

The way churches serve the poor and bring development that transforms is through their people. Different people in the church have different roles.

> **Our actions are evidence of our beliefs.**

1. What can pastors do to encourage their churches to foster development that transforms?

Pastors are very busy preaching, teaching, counseling, and working with other pastors. Pastors cannot do everything by themselves, so it's important for them to delegate and share responsibilities with others in the church. Church members also need to do the work of the church.

There are many other leaders in the church besides the pastor. There are lay leaders—Sunday school teachers, deacons, choir leaders, and also all the members of the church.

2. What are ways other leaders and people in the congregation can get involved in this work of development and transformation?

God's Word reminds us that our churches are filled with multiple "resources"—individuals with different gifts to be used for God's glory in the world.

> For just as each of us has one body with many members, and these members do not all have the same function, so in Christ we, though many, form one body, and each member belongs to all the others. We have different gifts, according to the grace given to each of us. (Romans 12:4-6)

As a Christian organization, World Relief aims to equip and empower the church to serve vulnerable people and transform communities. The church is God's chosen instrument for changing the world—caring for the poor and needy.

●◆ Review

- In what ways are the people of a congregation one of the greatest strengths of a church?

- How can your church care for the poor and needy in your community?

- Why is it important for the entire church to engage in development ministries?

◇ Reflect

Take a few moments to think about the strengths people have in your church. Think about how your church could do something to help people who are vulnerable and suffering in your community. Decide to talk with someone in your church about your idea.

ten

REFLECTION AND REVIEW

✔ Objectives

- Review some of the key points learned over the entire curriculum.
- Determine what personal commitments and actions to take to help and serve others.
- Consider how the church can help others in the community.

Looking Back

Here is an opportunity to look back at all you have learned in these sessions.

1 Understanding Development

1. What is development?

2. What are the different areas of development?

2 Understanding Poverty

3. In what ways can a person be poor or in need?

4. What is the origin of poverty in the world?

5. What is God's plan to rescue people from the effects of disobedience and sin?

3 God's Compassion for the Poor

6. What are some of the good gifts that God has given us to help us have a better life?

7. What does God say about people who oppress the poor?

4 The Transformation Tree

8. What is transformation?

9. How does the transformation tree represent transformation within us?

5 Development and Transformation

10. How do our beliefs and values determine the "fruit" in our lives, both good and bad? Give an example.

11. What does God say we must do to have much fruit in our lives (see John 15:5-8)?

6 Harmful Beliefs and Poverty

12. How do our beliefs contribute to poverty and suffering?

13. How can we overcome Satan's harmful lies that many people believe?

7 Replacing Harmful Beliefs with God's Truth

14. Why is it important to examine all of our beliefs and actions?

15. What is the role of churches in correcting harmful beliefs?

8 Relationships and Transformation

16. How does Jesus' story of the good Samaritan teach us how to respond to people in need?

17. How can healing relationships between people contribute to reducing poverty and improving the lives of the poor?

9 The Church and Poverty

18. Why should churches be involved in caring for the poor and needy in their communities?

19. Why is it important for more people than the pastor to become involved in a church's development ministries?

Biblical Reflection

All through this study, we were guided and informed by God's Word as to how we can stand with the vulnerable, whether in our own communities or around the world. We have seen how what we believe and value directly impacts how we act and respond, resulting in the corresponding outcomes. This includes our beliefs about the poor, the vulnerable, the purpose of Jesus' mission, and our individual roles as well as our corporate role as the church in serving God's purposes. This was not primarily a study about strategies to serve the poor or how to do good development work but rather understanding these matters in the light of God's Word and how that enables us to serve him better. Together we are called to love God with all our heart and to love our neighbors as ourselves. Spend some time on the following verses again and reflect on what they are saying. The stronger you believe in these truths, the better you will be able to serve God and the poor and vulnerable for whom he has such compassion.

> On one occasion an expert in the law stood up to test Jesus. "Teacher," he asked, "what must I do to inherit eternal life?"
>
> "What is written in the Law?" he replied. "How do you read it?"
>
> He answered, "'Love the Lord your God with all your heart and with all your soul and with all your strength and with all your mind'; and, 'Love your neighbor as yourself.'"
>
> "You have answered correctly," Jesus replied. "Do this and you will live." (Luke 10:25-28)

1. How does this passage define development that transforms?

> Whoever claims to love God yet hates a brother or sister is a liar. For whoever does not love their brother and sister, whom they have seen, cannot love God, whom they have not seen. (1 John 4:20)

2. What does this passage teach us regarding our relationship with God and our relationship with our neighbors?

I planted the seed, Apollos watered it, but God has been making it grow. So neither the one who plants nor the one who waters is anything, but only God, who makes things grow. The one who plants and the one who waters have one purpose, and they will each be rewarded according to their own labor. (1 Corinthians 3:6-8)

3. What do you learn about development in this passage?

"You will not certainly die," the serpent said to the woman. "For God knows that when you eat from it your eyes will be opened, and you will be like God, knowing good and evil."

When the woman saw that the fruit of the tree was good for food and pleasing to the eye, and also desirable for gaining wisdom, she took some and ate it. She also gave some to her husband, who was with her, and he ate it. Then the eyes of both of them were opened, and they realized they were naked; so they sewed fig leaves together and made coverings for themselves.

Then the man and his wife heard the sound of the LORD God as he was walking in the garden in the cool of the day, and they hid from the LORD God among the trees of the garden. But the LORD God called to the man, "Where are you?"

He answered, "I heard you in the garden, and I was afraid because I was naked; so I hid."

And he said, "Who told you that you were naked? Have you eaten from the tree that I commanded you not to eat from?"

The man said, "The woman you put here with me—she gave me some fruit from the tree, and I ate it."

Then the LORD God said to the woman, "What is this you have done?"

The woman said, "The serpent deceived me, and I ate."

So the LORD God said to the serpent, "Because you have done this,

"Cursed are you above all livestock
    and all wild animals!
You will crawl on your belly
    and you will eat dust
    all the days of your life.
And I will put enmity
    between you and the woman,
    and between your offspring and hers;
he will crush your head,
    and you will strike his heel."

To the woman he said,

> "I will make your pains in childbearing very severe;
>> with painful labor you will give birth to children.
> Your desire will be for your husband,
>> and he will rule over you."

To Adam he said, "Because you listened to your wife and ate fruit from the tree about which I commanded you, 'You must not eat from it,'

> "Cursed is the ground because of you;
>> through painful toil you will eat food from it
>> all the days of your life.
> It will produce thorns and thistles for you,
>> and you will eat the plants of the field.
> By the sweat of your brow
>> you will eat your food
> until you return to the ground,
>> since from it you were taken;
> for dust you are
>> and to dust you will return." (Genesis 3:4-19)

4. What do we learn about the relationship between the fall and suffering?

Which of you, if your son asks for bread, will give him a stone? Or if he asks for a fish, will give him a snake? If you, then, though you are evil, know how to give good gifts to your children, how much more will your Father in heaven give good gifts to those who ask him! (Matthew 7:9-11)

5. Why should we trust God and believe that he will provide good things for us?

Whoever oppresses the poor shows contempt for their Maker,
  but whoever is kind to the needy honors God. (Proverbs 14:31)

6. What do we learn in this verse about honoring God?

Is not this the kind of fasting I have chosen:
to loose the chains of injustice
   and untie the cords of the yoke,
to set the oppressed free
   and break every yoke?
Is it not to share your food with the hungry
   and to provide the poor wanderer with shelter—
when you see the naked, to clothe them,
   and not to turn away from your own flesh and blood? (Isaiah 58:6-7)

7. What does God's Word say about what we are sent to do?

Then the King will say to those on his right, "Come, you who are blessed by my Father; take your inheritance, the kingdom prepared for you since the creation of the world. For I was hungry and you gave me something to eat, I was thirsty and you gave me something to drink, I was a stranger and you invited me in, I needed clothes and you clothed me, I was sick and you looked after me, I was in prison and you came to visit me."

Then the righteous will answer him, "Lord, when did we see you hungry and feed you, or thirsty and give you something to drink? When did we see you a stranger and invite you in, or needing clothes and clothe you? When did we see you sick or in prison and go to visit you?"

The King will reply, "Truly I tell you, whatever you did for one of the least of these brothers and sisters of mine, you did for me." (Matthew 25:34-40)

8. Why should we respond to the needs of the poor and oppressed?

No good tree bears bad fruit, nor does a bad tree bear good fruit. Each tree is recognized by its own fruit. People do not pick figs from thornbushes, or grapes from briers. A good man brings good things out of the good stored up in his heart, and an evil man brings evil things out of the evil stored up in his heart. For the mouth speaks what the heart is full of. (Luke 6:43-45)

9. What is the relationship between the contents of our hearts and what we say and do?

I am the vine; you are the branches. If you remain in me and I in you, you will bear much fruit; apart from me you can do nothing. If you do not remain in me, you are like a branch that is thrown away and withers; such branches are picked up, thrown into the fire and burned. If you remain in me and my words remain in you, ask whatever you wish, and it will be done for you. This is to my Father's glory, that you bear much fruit, showing yourselves to be my disciples. (John 15:5-8)

10. When we bear fruit, what does that reveal to others around us?

11. What are some ways you "remain" in Jesus?

Do not conform to the pattern of this world, but be transformed by the renewing of your mind. Then you will be able to test and approve what God's will is—his good, pleasing and perfect will. (Romans 12:2)

12. Why is the renewing of your mind important for understanding God's heart for the vulnerable?

13. How do you renew your mind?

The god of this age [Satan] has blinded the minds of unbelievers, so that they cannot see the light of the gospel that displays the glory of Christ, who is the image of God. (2 Corinthians 4:4)

14. What does the Bible say about Satan and his influence?

You, dear children, are from God and have overcome them [false spirits], because the one who is in you is greater than the one who is in the world. They are from the world and therefore speak from the viewpoint of the world, and the world listens to them. We are from God, and whoever knows God listens to us; but whoever is not from God does not listen to us. This is how we recognize the Spirit of truth and the spirit of falsehood. (1 John 4:4-6)

15. List the truths from this passage of Scripture that can help you counter the harmful beliefs in your community.

In reply Jesus said: "A man was going down from Jerusalem to Jericho, when he was attacked by robbers. They stripped him of his clothes, beat him and went away, leaving him half dead. A priest happened to be going down the same road, and when he saw the man, he passed by on the other side. So too, a Levite, when he came to the place and saw him, passed by on the other side. But a Samaritan, as he traveled, came where the man was; and when he saw him, he took pity on him. He went to him and bandaged his wounds, pouring on oil and wine. Then he put the man on his own donkey, brought him to an inn and took care of him. The next day he took out two denarii and gave them to the innkeeper. 'Look after him,' he said, 'and when I return, I will reimburse you for any extra expense you may have.'

"Which of these three do you think was a neighbor to the man who fell into the hands of robbers?"

The expert in the law replied, "The one who had mercy on him."

Jesus told him, "Go and do likewise." (Luke 10:30-37)

16. What are some reasons that we don't help others?

Love must be sincere. Hate what is evil; cling to what is good. Be devoted to one another in love. Honor one another above yourselves. Never be lacking in zeal, but keep your spiritual fervor, serving the Lord. Be joyful in hope, patient in affliction, faithful in prayer. Share with the Lord's people who are in need. Practice hospitality.

Bless those who persecute you; bless and do not curse. Rejoice with those who rejoice; mourn with those who mourn. Live in harmony with one another. Do not be proud, but be willing to associate with people of low position. Do not be conceited.

Do not repay anyone evil for evil. Be careful to do what is right in the eyes of everyone. If it is possible, as far as it depends on you, live at peace with everyone. (Romans 12:9-18)

17. How does God want us to respond to those who mistreat us, and how does he want us to relate and respond to people in need?

And if you spend yourselves in behalf of the hungry
    and satisfy the needs of the oppressed,
then your light will rise in the darkness,
    and your night will become like the noonday.
The LORD will guide you always;
    he will satisfy your needs in a sun-scorched land
    and will strengthen your frame.
You will be like a well-watered garden,
    like a spring whose waters never fail. (Isaiah 58:10-11)

18. What do we learn in this passage about caring for the poor and vulnerable?

The Spirit of the Lord is on me,
    because he has anointed me
    to proclaim good news to the poor.
He has sent me to proclaim freedom for the prisoners
    and recovery of sight for the blind,
to set the oppressed free,
    to proclaim the year of the Lord's favor. (Luke 4:18-19)

19. What was the purpose of Jesus' ministry?

What good is it, my brothers and sisters, if someone claims to have faith but has no deeds? Can such faith save them? Suppose a brother or a sister is without clothes and daily food. If one of you says to them, "Go in peace; keep warm and well fed," but does nothing about their physical needs, what good is it? In the same way, faith by itself, if it is not accompanied by action, is dead. (James 2:14-17)

20. According to this passage, what does a person with living faith look like?

Personal Reflection

With this in mind, think back to those hopes and dreams you thought about in the first session.

1. What are the dreams, the fruit, that you hope for in your life?

2. Think about how to reach these dreams. Are there values and beliefs that you need to change for this to happen?

3. What actions will you take to reach your dreams?

Reflecting on Relationships

As we change in our personal lives, our relationships will also be transformed.

1. How would you like your relationships to change within your family? Your community? Your church? With God?

2. What changes would you like to see in your community and church?

3. What will you do differently to love others as part of loving God?

4. How will you help your church and community take action?

Finishing the Story

We have been following the story of Sarah's family. In session eight, we heard how Sarah and John's neighbors, Elizabeth and Jacob, were reaching out to them. Elizabeth invited Sarah to a health group at her church. Jacob invited John to attend trainings that would help improve his productivity and livelihood.

There are many different ways that Elizabeth, Jacob, and the local church might help Sarah and John. In the same way, there are many different things our own churches can do.

1. Imagine people in your own community like Sarah and John. Based on the strengths and resources identified in our church congregations and communities, what actions can be taken to help them?

There are many different good things we can do! There are many different ways to help. Let us begin taking steps to love our neighbors and help them.

ACKNOWLEDGMENTS

The curriculum that this book is based on is the product of practitioners and implementers from many countries on four continents, including Megan Laughlin, Susan Conway, Dennis Mwangwela, Myal Green, Emmanuel Ngoga, Maurice Kwizera, Debbie Dortzbach, Stephan Bauman, Gary Fairchild, Muriel Elmer, and Laura Van Vuuren, within the World Relief family.

The hand illustration, as far as it can be known, originated with Ted Ward in the 1970s and was slightly modified by Karl Dortzbach. The Transformation Tree concept originated with Darrow Miller and the organization Disciple the Nations and was modified by Medical Ambassadors International under the guidance of Stan Rowland.

The stories of Sarah and John and the other characters used in this curriculum are composites of situations that World Relief experiences and confronts in the regions where we work. These individuals are the real heroes of this work as they allow the truth of God's Word to replace false beliefs in their lives, resulting in real-life transformation. It is people like Sarah and John who have been instrumental in bringing spiritual and physical change to their communities.

Without the professional editorial services of InterVarsity Press under the guidance of Al Hsu, this project would never have been completed. I am deeply indebted to them.

Finally, without the intervening work of the Holy Spirit, this would simply be a good exercise in awareness and learning. Only God can bring lasting transformation to individuals and communities. Therefore prayer is not preparation for embarking on this study, but prayer is the indispensable means through which these concepts can become a reality in the lives of the readers and their communities.

LEADER'S NOTES

Standing with the Vulnerable is for the church, the body of Christ. Our hope is that it will spur on your local church to be an agent of transformation in your community—to initiate and participate in life-changing ministry.

Each session incorporates biblical truths with development concepts and is designed to encourage group dialogue and reflection. Our desire for this curriculum is that it would mobilize the church to engage in the great causes of our day, and that the church would regard this engagement as an inseparable dimension of our witness of Jesus Christ as Lord and Savior.

We also affirm that prayer is not preparation for the battle—prayer *is* the battle. We trust that those who use this manual will be committed to prayer.

The material that follows includes suggestions for how to lead a group through this study. It offers many ideas for materials to bring, how to prepare, how to review the previous session (suggested language is in *italics*), group activities, and suggested responses to the discussion questions. (Note that not every discussion question has a response.)

May you be strengthened by God's unfailing love and guided by his Spirit as you facilitate these sessions!

Tips for Leading

Be Prepared. Complete the entire session in advance. Any topics or questions that you find difficult are likely to come up in discussion with the group. If you have a white board or flip-chart paper available, you can write out Scripture verses and questions, or re-create the images or charts in advance.

Be a Good Listener. As the facilitator, you need to encourage discussion. That means no single person should dominate the conversation—including you. Allow participants time to answer questions, encourage them to share ideas and affirm their responses.

Be Yourself. You don't have to have all the right answers. Your responsibility is to help the participants learn well and to make them want to keep coming back. Remember, the more relaxed you are, the more comfortable others will be.

Pray. Prayer is vital. Spend time in prayer as you prepare to lead each session, open and close each session in prayer, and invite others—friends and church members—to be in prayer for your group.

Session 1

Purpose: The purpose of the first session is to introduce participants to some of the main ideas in this curriculum. This session contains an overview of development and how we can grow and develop into the people God intended us to be. It is very important to help people feel welcome. It is also very important that people enjoy themselves.

Materials Needed

- A small seed, preferably one that grows into a large plant or tree (whatever seeds you have in your region), and an extra chair or bench.

Helpful Hints

- Be sure to plan for a fifteen-minute break somewhere in the middle of the session. A break will help the participants to feel refreshed and pay better attention to the last half of the session. Practice the development game ahead of time so you are ready to lead it with the group.

Discussion Questions

Developing the Whole Person

1. Food, water, safety, rest

3. Soil, sun, water, protection

4. It sprouts and then puts out shoots that grow into roots and seedlings. A trunk and branches form, and eventually it will produce fruit.

5. Tree, bush, plant, etc.

Growing as a Whole Person

1. He was healed physically because his leg was healed, but he wasn't healed emotionally because he planned to hurt his neighbor.

2. Emotional hurts can be the result of fear, lack of trust, ignorance, or inaccurate beliefs.

3. Wrong beliefs result in wrongful actions.

4. The child can pay attention and learn better (mental).

5. She is hopeful because she knows God loves her, she sees herself as worthy and special because she is made in the image of God (emotional).

6. It is hard to think and do well in school (mental).

7. He may be shunned (social); he will be discouraged (emotional).

The Greatest Commandment

1. Emotional (love God with your heart); mental (with your mind); physical (with your strength); social (love your neighbor); choices (choosing to do what God says).

2. We are to love God with every area of our lives. Since every area of life is spiritual, we choose whether or not to serve God with every aspect of life.

3. God views each of us as a whole person and considers every aspect of life significant. Our growth should move us toward loving God more.

The Needs and Strengths of a Family

1. Physical—the family does not have enough food, John has a disability, they are not earning enough money to send all the children to school; mental—Sarah has little education and cannot read or write, not all the children are in school; social—they fight with a family from a neighboring village and experience discrimination because of their lack of resources; emotional—Sarah worries about feeding and educating their family, John does not feel safe and is afraid of the family that beat him; good choices—Sarah believes she cannot make good choices so she seeks advice from others; spiritual—Sarah does not know God.

2. Physical—the family has their own house and land, and they are hard workers; mental—two children are in school; social—they get along well with their neighbors and talk about their problems together; emotional—they are happy together as a family; good choices—they are sending their children to school, John has chosen to be faithful to Sarah; spiritual—Sarah has an awareness of God, she is happy when she attends church.

Application Activity: Development Game (15 minutes)

Ask for five volunteers. Have them stand next to one another in front of the main group. Also have one empty chair or bench up front near the volunteers.

• Say to the volunteers: *All of you together represent one person. You represent a young man named Peter. Each of you represents a different area of Peter's development.*

• Say to one volunteer: *You represent Peter's **physical** well-being. He suffers from poor nutrition and is sick a lot. To represent this, you must keep one arm behind your back.*

- Say to the next volunteer: *You represent Peter's **mental** well-being—his mind. He has had few opportunities to learn and cannot read. To represent this problem in his life, you can only use your left leg.*

- Say to the next volunteer: *You represent Peter's **emotional** well-being. Peter is very sad and angry all the time. He has no hope for the future—he believes that a man like him will never amount to anything. To represent this, you can only use your right leg.*

- Say to the next volunteer: *You represent Peter's **social** well-being. He works very hard and spends no time with friends or family. He is very lonely. To represent this, you cannot move at all—you are paralyzed.*

- Say to the next volunteer: *You represent Peter's need to **make healthy choices**. Peter feels very helpless. He does not think his life can make a difference. To represent this, you must keep both arms behind your back.*

- Say to all the volunteers: *In addition, all of you are part of Peter's **spiritual** well-being. Peter does not follow Christ with his life. To represent this, all of you must also close your eyes.*

- Say to all: *Remember you are all ONE person. And Peter must try to get through his daily life. To represent this, you must all work together to move this chair across the room.*

Let them try. Remind them that they must work together since they are one person. It will be very difficult for them.

- If the group fails call them all back to where they started and say, *Let's try it again. This time, you are still one person, Peter. But now imagine these needs have been met in Peter's life. He has had good development in his physical, mental, emotional, and social areas and in making healthy choices. He loves God with his whole life. You have no limitations this time. You can use all arms, legs, and eyes. Now try to move the chair.*

Let them try. This time it will be very easy. Thank the volunteers for helping with the activity. Then ask the group the following questions:

- *How was it when you tried to move the chair the first time?*

- *And how was it the second time?*

- *What does this teach us about the importance of meeting all areas of need in a person's life?* [Unmet needs hold them back; all areas must work together with the others; if there is a problem in one area, it will slow the other areas down.]

Session 2

Purpose: The purpose of the session is for people to think of poverty in a new way. This session will also help participants understand what the Bible says about poverty. Just as in session one, it is very important that people feel free to speak openly and honestly. We want people to enjoy themselves as they are learning.

Helpful Hints

- This session offers a lot of information. It will make learning more effective for participants to discuss concepts together in small groups of four or five people. If you are creative, practice telling the stories in an interesting way, with different tones of voice, so it is easy for people to engage with the story. Be ready with examples of different levels of poverty from local contexts so that participants can see that there are some people in the community in extreme need. Feel free to adapt all the examples to your local context.

Welcome and Review

Welcome participants and share the learning objectives for today's session.

Before we begin today's session, let's review what we learned in our previous session.

- *What does the word* development *mean?* [to grow, the process of growing or improving]

- *What are the areas of a person's life that need to develop and grow?* (Encourage participants to use their hands to help them remember.) [physical, mental, emotional, social, making choices, and spiritual]

- *What areas of a person's life are controlled by the spiritual?* [ALL parts of life are spiritual. God created us this way and wants us to love him with our whole self.]

- *At the end of session one we were asked to identify our strengths in each of the areas of development. Turn to the person next to you and take a few minutes to share the strengths you each identified.*

We can find strengths in ourselves if we look for them. It might be surprising how many strengths we can find in our lives.

Discussion Questions

The Origins of Poverty

1. God said that it was good.

2. God made man and woman in his own image.

3. They were partners. Adam and Eve both needed each other and both were blessed by God. God instructed them to "be fruitful and multiply." God gave Adam and Eve the Garden of Eden for food. Their job was to work the land and protect the garden.

4. God had a close relationship with Adam and Eve. They walked and talked together.

5. Physical—plants for food, safety, shelter; emotional—created by and loved by God; social—they needed each other, they were partners; mental—God gave tasks that used their mind and creativity, tending the garden and naming the animals;

good choices—God gave them the ability to make good choices, he gave them guidelines; spiritual—they had a close relationship with God, they talked to him.

The Fall and Poverty

1. The serpent told Eve that she would not die if she ate fruit from the tree.

2. Yes. They believed Satan's lie and disobeyed God, and then they ate the fruit from the tree of the knowledge of good and evil.

3. Adam and Eve became ashamed of themselves because they saw they were naked; they hid from God.

4. Eve—In addition to having difficulties in childbirth, God also told Eve that there would be conflicts in her relationship with Adam. Adam—God told Adam that instead of the enjoyable work he was doing in the garden, his work would become hard. Despite Adam's efforts, the ground would not produce much food.

5. Cain killed his brother.

6. They lost the close relationship with God; they were separated from him.

7. There was conflict between Adam and Eve, including blame and shame. This led to conflict in their family when Cain murdered Abel out of anger and jealousy.

8. The soil no longer produced much food to eat, and work became difficult. Adam and Eve had to leave the safety of the garden. Childbirth became much more dangerous and painful.

9. God and people: not knowing God's love; not praying to him for help; not trusting God or believing his promises and truths; worshiping other gods and spirits with fear; paying traditional healers for help; lacking hope; becoming bitter and not trying to improve.

    People: fighting and war; corrupt leaders who do not help their people; violence in families; abuse of children; husbands who leave their wives and children; cheating to make more money; the powerful taking advantage of the weak.

    People and creation: crops failing; unclean water that causes diseases; standing water that increases mosquitoes; natural disasters such as floods or earthquakes; dumping trash and polluting the environment; deforestation.

A Very Sad Day for Sarah

1. There was a lack of money to go to the clinic, lack of transportation, and lack of knowledge about what to do.

2. Sarah took the advice of her grandmother and went to the traditional healer

instead; she did not know her son needed immediate treatment at the clinic; the clinic was far away.

3. Sarah used traditional healing rituals; she doubted God's love and felt abandoned by him.

4. The clinic nurse blamed Sarah and was unkind in her grief.

5. The village had a problem with mosquitoes that caused Sarah's baby to get malaria and die; the land does not produce much food.

God's Rescue Plan for the World

1. God's love for us is so great that he gave his only son, Jesus, to die for us.

2. He will forgive our sins against him and make us his children—a part of God's family!

Session 3

Purpose: The purpose of the session is to help participants better understand God's compassion for the poor and to reflect on how God's church can show compassion to people in need in their communities. Just as in session two, it is very important that people feel free to share their thoughts openly and honestly.

Helpful Hints

- This session offers a lot of information. During discussions, allow participants to reflect and ask questions. It will also make learning more effective if participants can discuss concepts together in pairs or small groups of 4-5 people.

Welcome and Review

Welcome participants and share the learning objectives for today's session.

Before we begin today's session, let's review what we learned in our previous session. We discussed how sin and suffering came into the world when Adam and Eve intentionally disobeyed God.

- *What happened to Adam and Eve's relationships with God and each other when they sinned?* [Their relationship with God was broken. They began to experience conflict and hate in their relationships with each other.]

- *What happened to the relationship between Adam and Eve and the world God created after they sinned?* [The land produced less, growing food became difficult. Life was hard. Disease and death became common.]

We talked about how these broken relationships increase suffering. We also discussed the different ways a person can be poor.

- *In addition to lacking resources, what are other ways a person can be poor?* [Physically—sickness, disease; socially—through broken relationships with others; emotionally—by not trusting God or believing his truths and promises, being filled with fear; mentally—by not having an education or responsibilities; making good choices: by choosing harmful beliefs over God's truths; spiritually: by denying God and worshiping other gods, following harmful beliefs.]

When God created men and women, he made them in his very own image. When Adam and Eve disobeyed their maker, the image of God in them was distorted but not destroyed. God still loves the world and the people in it. Ever since human beings and all of creation were altered by sin, God has been at work restoring creation and reconciling people to himself. In fact, Colossians 1:20 reminds us that through Jesus, God is reconciling "to himself all things, whether things on earth or things in heaven."
We called this God's "rescue plan" for us.

- *Because God loves us and wants to restore the broken relationship caused by sin, what did he do for us?* [God sent his son Jesus to die for our sins so that he could restore his relationship with us. Jesus rose from the dead; he is alive today!]

If you believe in Jesus and have already accepted him into your life, we asked you to thank him for saving you and to ask him to show you how you can join in loving and caring for the people around you.

- *Who can share about their story of reconciliation?*

If you have more questions about how to pray and join in this relationship with God, please speak with me at the end of the session or meet with your pastor to discuss this.

Discussion Questions

God's Good Gifts

1. Annie recovered because Sarah made a good decision and acted quickly; Sarah learned that going to the traditional healer didn't help her son.

2. God provides people, good information, skills, and medicines to help us.

3. We are God's children; he loves us and wants the best for us.

4. Laws that protect us, hospitals and clinics, church programs that aid those in need, aide organizations, government programs that help those in need.

The Suffering of the Poor

1. Theft, lack of savings, a heartless moneylender, greed, fear.

2. Anger of the ancestors, sin, curses.

Caring for the Needs of Others

1. We need to do things to help others in need—take action—not just wish them well.

2. When we help others we honor God.

Who Are the Most Vulnerable?

1. Grace. She has more money and a nicer house.

2. Sarah, because she has a good marriage. The relationship between Grace and her husband is violent.

3. Probably Sarah's family, because there is no violence in the home. Both Grace and her children are very afraid and unhappy.

Table 1

	Characteristics of those who are well-off and flourishing	Characteristics of those who are needy or impoverished
emotional	Peace, hope, good self-esteem	Easily angered, fearful, worry
mental	Educated, skilled	Little or no education, cannot read, few life skills
physical	Have housing, sufficient food and clothing	Lack adequate shelter, food, clothing
social	Supportive extended family or community	Orphaned or widowed with no extended family support
good choices	Feel empowered, realistic, make decisions to help have a better future	Feel unable to make a difference, might not think they have a choice
spiritual	Trust God, take problems to God, willing to help others	Don't know God or have a relationship with him, do not have peace

Session 4

Purpose: This session introduces another main concept of the curriculum: transformation. It also brings together the ideas of development and transformation, using the picture of the tree to aid understanding. As the facilitator you will need to help participants understand how changes in their beliefs, values, thinking, and attitudes (their inward self) relate to changes in their actions, behaviors, choices, and results of their actions (their outward self).

Helpful Hints

- Personal transformation is a very important—and sometimes difficult—idea to understand. Practice explaining the transformation tree ahead of time, pointing to different parts of the tree as you explain them. Be enthusiastic as you go through this session with participants and engage them as much as possible during the session to help them better understand these concepts.

Welcome and Review

Before we begin today's session, let's review what we learned in our previous session when we talked about the good gifts God gives us.

- *What were some of the good gifts we receive from a good God?* [sunshine, rain, medicine, food, shelter]

We learned about God's compassion for the poor and needy and what God thinks of those who oppress the poor.

- *What is God's response to those who oppress the poor?* [God says they show contempt for (him) their maker; they demean and dishonor God himself.]

In the Bible we saw that God expects us, his children, to care for the poor and needy around us.

- *What are some things God tells the church to do for the poor?* [Feed the hungry, stand for the vulnerable, help them grow spiritually.]

At the end of our last session, we asked you to speak with someone you considered to be poor and to learn more about how they see themselves and their day-to-day life.

- *What are the very poor and vulnerable people like in our community?*

In our first session, we realized that God wants us to grow. We used the word development to mean "the process of growth and positive change." We talked about how God created us, with different needs for growth.

- *What are the areas where we need to grow?* [physically, mentally, socially, emotionally, and making choices]

And our entire lives are influenced by how we love God (the spiritual). We have said that just as our fingers and palm are part of one hand, all of our needs are linked together. Imagine if only one finger were to grow on a hand! It would not be very useful. In the same way it is important that all areas of our lives grow together.

In our first session, we talked about how growth and development happen and how a large tree begins with a small seed.

Today, we will use the transformation tree to help us understand how growth happens in our lives. We will use the parts of a tree to show the connection between what we believe, or what we think is true; and what we value, what we think is important or best.

We will also look at how these beliefs and values influence our actions and behaviors and lead to the consequences of our choices, or the results of our actions and behaviors.

Discussion Questions

The Transformation Tree

1. Roots

2. Trunk

3. Branches

4. Leaves/Fruit

5. The entire tree will be weak, there will be no fruit, and the wind could blow it over.

6. It will grow well, have a strong trunk and branches, and produce abundant leaves, flowers, and fruit.

A Family Transformed

1. All children are created in God's image and are gifts from him, so parents are responsible for their children's care as they develop.

2. They value healthy practices they learned from health workers, including providing good nutrition, clean water, hygiene, and disease prevention.

3. Elizabeth breastfeeds her babies and gives them good nutrition. Elizabeth has implemented the health practices she has learned and is willing to go to the clinic when necessary.

4. Their children are healthy and growing well.

Bearing Good Fruit

1. If we have a good heart, we will have good fruit. It is not possible to have good fruit in our lives if inside we remain full of darkness and evil.

2. The snake only made small surface changes, but the caterpillar was transformed from inside.

Growth That Brings Transformation

1. The spiritual, our relationship with God.

2. Our growth and transformation begin with our "roots": believing the truth.

3. Our values begin to change our actions, and this leads to good fruit.

The Transformation of Sarah's Neighbor

1. She believed she couldn't save and that she would never have enough money.

2. She believed that she could save money, that God loved her, that she had talents, and that she could learn.

3. They helped her to persevere even when it was difficult to keep saving money and encouraged her to learn more and help others.

4. Elizabeth grew closer to God, improved her mind, and showed love to her neighbor by helping Sarah's family.

Application Activity: Create a Song

We have been learning many different ideas. Today, we will do an activity that will help us find a good way to remember these things.

Divide the group into two teams and say, *Your task is to create a song. Each group will get a different idea to put into a song. Be creative—add actions or a dance if you wish! The first group will create a song about transformation—how God's love for us changes what we believe, our values, our behaviors, and our actions. The second group will create a song about how God's commandment that we love him and love our neighbors changes our churches, our homes, and our communities. You will have about fifteen minutes to prepare your song. Then we will perform for one another.*

Let each group move to a different part of a room or even to a different space outside so each team has enough space to prepare. After fifteen minutes, gather the whole group together. Let each group perform, and then have everyone sing the songs together.

Session 5

Purpose: This session builds participants' understanding of development that transforms people and communities by helping them apply the model of the transformation tree—beliefs, values, behaviors/actions, and results—to everyday situations. This session will help participants recognize that people's beliefs influence what they value and how they think and act. It may be difficult for participants to understand the connections at first, so take plenty of time to review the transformation tree.

Helpful Hints

- Feel free to adjust the names and details in the stories about Sarah and her friends to fit your local context. Just be sure every story you use includes an example of beliefs influencing values, values leading to action, and specific actions leading to results.

Welcome and Review

Before we begin today's session, let's review what we learned in our previous session. We learned about the process of transformation and used a picture of a tree to help us understand how growth and change happen in our lives.

Ask for a volunteer to place the labels on the tree; be sure they are in the correct places.

- *Who can place the labels on the tree and explain what the parts represent?* [roots—our beliefs—what we believe is true; trunk—our values—what we think is important or best; branches—our actions—what we do and say; fruit—the results—what is seen, what happens as a result of our actions]

- *Where does transformation that brings good results start?* [with our beliefs]

Application Activity: Explaining the Tree to Others

Participants will form pairs for this activity.

I hope you are enjoying what we are learning during our time together. We do not want this learning to stop here! We want you to teach others, too. Everyone find a partner to work with for this activity. The purpose of this activity is to begin practicing how to teach others about the transformation tree.

Hand out a flip-chart page and marker to each person.

First, every person will draw a transformation tree. The picture that we have been using can help guide you. Make sure the tree you draw has roots, trunk, branches, and fruit—all the parts you will need in order to talk about the model of development that transforms us.

Then, practice explaining the model of transformation to one another, using the tree you have drawn. Imagine that your partner has never heard of this before and you are the first one to tell them about this. Use your picture to help you explain about beliefs, values, behaviors, and results. You can also use some of the stories as examples. Take a few minutes to draw your trees. Then take turns explaining the tree to one another.

Let participants ask any questions they have. After all have practiced explaining the tree to each other in pairs, ask the group:

- *How did the transformation tree help you share what you learned?*

- *What was the easiest part of explaining the transformation tree?*

- *What was the most difficult part of explaining the transformation tree?*

Discussion Questions

Understanding Transformation from Within

1. Enrolling a child in school, supporting the child throughout the school years, encouraging the child.

2. The parents think that schooling is best for their child; they value their child and want the child to complete schooling and develop mentally.

3. God has created us with the ability to learn many things; growing mentally can bring a good life.

4. Education is not a good investment; people don't need to develop mentally and learn many things; a child does not need education to have a good life.

5. That child will not get a good job or develop their potential; the uneducated are more vulnerable and will not be able to teach their own children well.

Understanding the Transformation Tree

Table 2

	Jacob and Elizabeth	Elizabeth	Daniel	Daniel and Agnes
What is seen: Results	Safe delivery of healthy child.	Less child sickness and death in community.	A good crop; pleases God by caring for his creation.	Widows and orphans are able to keep their land and houses.
What is done: Behaviors/ Actions	Ensured good care for mother and baby, used money for clinic, both tested for HIV.	Attended training sessions; shares health lessons with other mothers, who follow her advice.	Practices crop rotation so the soil is not depleted or used up.	Work with their church to protect inheritance rights of widows and orphans.
What is best: Values	To protect wife and baby; to receive prenatal care; values the life of his child and wants to protect from HIV.	Values knowledge that will keep her children and other children in her community healthy.	Values training, values God's creation; best and important to care for the land.	Value widows and orphans, willing; best to protect the vulnerable.
What is true: Beliefs	All people are created equal. Women and children are as important to God as are men.	Children are a gift from God; health and development of children is important.	People are protectors of God's creation. It is important to care for the land.	God calls people to defend the rights of widows and orphans. All people deserve a safe place to live.

Physical: healthy women and children, less sickness, good crops, shelter for widows and orphans, being tested for HIV.

Mental: learning new information, sharing information with others.

Emotional: happy families.

Social: helping neighbors, sharing with others, building stronger families.

Good choices: seeking care from the clinic, healthy children, caring for the land.

Bearing Good Fruit

1. We cannot produce fruit on our own, so we need to stay connected to Jesus. Just as the branches need the vine, we need Jesus in order to bear fruit.

2. It reveals that we are Jesus' disciples.

3. Reading the Bible, praying, being faithful.

4. Good and plentiful fruit.

5. It helps us see the world in a new way, in a way that is pleasing to God; then our values and our actions will be based on God's truth.

Session 6

Purpose: This session continues to build on the idea that what we believe in our hearts and minds determines how we grow. Our beliefs inform our values, which direct our actions, and our actions bring results. The closer our beliefs and values align with God's word and truth, the easier it is to act in ways that are pleasing to God and to bear good fruit. However, when our beliefs are based on harmful or ungodly values, our actions will follow with negative outcomes or bitter fruit. In this session, we focus on these negative outcomes—signs of "poverty" in our lives. It is important for participants to understand that our beliefs can bring either good or ill results. It all starts with what we think in our hearts and minds.

Helpful Hints

- Adapt the stories and all examples of traditional beliefs to what is common in your local community. Remember that you will not change people's minds all at once—it takes time to change deeply held traditional beliefs and convictions. Your role as the facilitator is to encourage participants to start the process of seeing the world in a new way and living in a way that is pleasing to God, by examining whether these beliefs bring good results or deepen poverty.

Welcome and Review

Before we begin today's session, let's review what we learned in our previous session. During the previous session we focused on biblical truths, how they affect what we think is best, and how that can lead us to positive actions and behaviors and good results.

- *Were you able to tell someone else about how transformation can happen, using the tree? What was it like to do that—who did you talk to? What was this person's reaction to what you shared?*

Let people share their experiences if they had an opportunity to do it.

In Elizabeth and Jacob's story we saw how their marriage was transformed because they believed God's truth about marriage. We also saw how we can be transformed in all areas of our lives. We learned how our beliefs help us decide what we will value, and how what we value leads to our actions. Our actions then lead to results we can see in our lives.

- *What are some of the other fruits of development that transforms?* [Mothers have healthy babies; husbands and wives have good relationships; widows keep their property.]

Discussion Questions

A Strong Marriage

1. They believe that God commands men and women to be faithful in marriage.

2. They think it is important to live by God's commands, his truths.

3. They remain faithful to each other even when tempted not to do so.

4. They trust each other, they have a strong marriage, and they do not have HIV/ AIDS or other sexually transmissible diseases.

Poverty and the Transformation Tree

1. Trees in soil fertilized with lies are barren and/or dead; trees in soil fertilized with some truth show some life and vigor.

2. The more truth in the soil fertilizing the trees, the stronger the tree.

3. People can be divided by believing lies; lies can cause mistrust and conflict; lies result in harmful behaviors.

Satan, the Father of Lies

1. He is a liar, and blinds the minds of unbelievers. This encourages unhealthy, destructive behaviors or values.

2. He told Eve a lie, saying that they wouldn't die even though God said they would.

Lies That Lead to Bitter Fruit

1. She has less knowledge to pass on to her own children when she becomes a mother; she cannot read or get a good job to help support her family; she will be dependent on her husband; she may not know her legal rights or be able to defend herself if she is exploited or abused; she may lack self-confidence and think she cannot improve her life.

2. Her parents spent money on her brother's education but did not invest in her education; she was kept at home.

3. They think girls are not worth the money for education.

4. They believe that boys are better than girls—they are not equal. The harmful lie is that girls are not worth the trouble of paying for their education.

5. Countries that do not educate their females continue to struggle economically and politically.

6. He values his own life and health more than that of a little girl.

7. His actions will be entirely self-serving; he will not care how his actions affect anyone else, especially not a little girl.

8. The infected men remain HIV positive *and* they infect many younger girls with the disease. These girls may also become pregnant and then their babies might contract HIV/AIDS. These young girls are injured physically and emotionally, they feel used and discarded, and often drop out of school.

9. No money for emergencies, medicines, school fees, etc.

10. The man spent his money on roasted meat in the market or alcohol instead of saving it.

11. The man's own desires are more important than the welfare of his family.

12. He has no hope for changing or improving his life, so he lives for himself and his own enjoyment of the present.

Session 7

Purpose: In this session, we focus on some of the harmful beliefs that result in bitter fruit—signs of "poverty" in our lives. It is important for participants to understand that our beliefs can bring either good or ill results. It all starts with what we believe in our hearts and minds. The work of the church is to counter these harmful beliefs with God's truth and trust in his power to help us.

Helpful Hints

- The stories and examples of traditional beliefs can be adapted to what is common in your local community. Your role as the facilitator is to encourage participants to start the process of seeing the world in a new way and living in a way that is pleasing to God, by examining whether these beliefs bring good results or deepen poverty. Remember that you will not change people's minds all at once—it takes time to change deeply held traditional beliefs and convictions.

Welcome and Review

Welcome participants and share the learning objectives for today's session.

In our previous session we discussed the problem of how harmful beliefs destroy good development and transformation in our lives and in our communities. First we looked at three different trees.

Show the picture of the three trees.

- *What do you remember about these trees? Describe each one to us.* [The first tree is a very poor tree because it is rooted in many lies; the second tree is growing a little better because it is rooted in more truth, but there is only a small amount of fruit; the third tree is growing well because it is rooted almost completely in truth, and there is plenty of good fruit.]

- *What does the Bible say about Satan's plan?* [He is a liar and a deceiver.]

Point to the roots/beliefs of the transformation tree.

- *How do we overcome Satan's harmful lies that many people believe?* [By faithfully teaching God's truth from his Word, by trusting in his power over Satan, by being obedient to his teachings and following Jesus.]

- *Where do we get the power to stand against Satan's deception?* [From God himself and the power of his Holy Spirit.]

Ask someone to read aloud Ephesians 3:20-21: "Now to him who is able to do immeasurably more than all we ask or imagine, according to his power that is at work within us, to him be glory in the church and in Christ Jesus throughout all generations, for ever and ever! Amen!"

Discussion Questions

Traditional Beliefs

1. People want to avoid illness so they attempt to find a cause.

2. People avoid being outdoors in the cold weather, thinking that this will keep them healthier.

3. People still get sick since the cold virus is actually transmitted through human contact—whether outdoors in the cold weather or indoors in the warmth.

4. Parents don't want youth to be sexually active at a young age.

5. These parents avoid talking about the beauty of sex and intimacy.

6. Youth end up learning false lessons about sex from other sources—movies, internet, peers—instead of learning the truth from their parents.

How Some Traditional Beliefs Lead to Poverty

Table 3

Story	Beliefs	Values	Behavior (Actions)	Results (Consequences)
Grace's beliefs about diet during pregnancy	Pregnant women should not eat meat.	It's important to follow traditional beliefs and avoid having bad things happen during pregnancy.	Grace does not eat meat during her pregnancy.	Both Grace and her child are malnourished, so the baby was very weak when he was born.
Sarah and John's beliefs about curses	People can use spiritual powers to harm and curse one another.	Value traditional beliefs as more important than God's power to protect them	Sarah and John are suspicious of their neighbors and argue with them.	There is less support in the neighborhood for clean-up day. Sarah and John have bad relationships with their neighbors.
Beliefs about ancestors	Traditional spiritual practices are the most powerful source of help and protect a person from evil.	Value traditional beliefs as more important than God's power to protect them	Sarah spends her money on rituals instead of using it for family needs.	Sarah lacks money for things that would definitely benefit her family (fertilizer, the clinic), and the rituals do not bring a benefit.
Beliefs about HIV and AIDS	HIV and AIDS is caused by a curse.	Avoid people with HIV/AIDS so you are not also cursed.	John will not go to Martha's store and tells other people not to go there.	Martha becomes very poor and has to close her store from the lack of customers.

1. Family members, respected community leaders, friends.

2. If beliefs are harmful, we will be negatively affected; we should examine our beliefs and values to see which ones lead to positive change and which beliefs hold us back.

The Role of the Church

1. Even though we will face problems (hardship, persecution, famine, nakedness, danger, sword), they can never keep us from the love of God.

2. His love is greater than our problems and gives us the courage to take action.

3. Do not keep thinking in the same way as those who do not fear God. Our minds should be renewed and changed.

4. Renewing our minds means having new beliefs and values in line with what Christ teaches us. It means we are able to think more like Christ and that we leave behind our old, negative beliefs and values.

5. We can use our reason to think and test so we see what is God's will; this will change our values and our behaviors.

Transformation in Communities

1. God created women in his image; men and women are equal before God and equally loved by him

3. The One who is in us (God) is greater than the one in the world (Satan); whoever knows God listens to us; we can recognize truth and falsehood.

Session 8

Purpose: The purpose of this session is for participants to understand that development that transforms us is more than just an individual effort. True change demands healing our relationships with God, with other people, and with creation. This session reviews how poverty has affected these relationships and then uses the story of the good Samaritan to illustrate how transformed people take action to love their neighbors. Restoring our relationships is an essential part of development that transforms.

Helpful Hints

- Feel free to adapt stories to fit your local context. Keep the emphasis on transformed people reaching out to help others.

Welcome and Review

Welcome participants and share the learning objectives for today's session.

In the previous session we talked about the negative results of poverty.

- *Why is it important that we examine our beliefs and values when we consider these negative results?* [Our beliefs and values determine our actions; some beliefs are harmful and lead to bad results; some can be lies planted by Satan to deceive us.]

As Christians, we believe it is best when our roots, our beliefs, are planted in the truths of Jesus. If you see good "fruit," you know you have good "roots." When you created your transformation trees in our previous session, you considered a problem, or negative fruit, and then identified what the underlying beliefs and values were, along with the outward actions that led to this problem.

- *Who can name one of these beliefs and then share the biblical truth that replaced this lie of Satan?*

• *Did any of you tell someone about a harmful belief and replace it with God's truth? If so, who could share their experience?*

Let several participants share their experiences.

Application Activity: Healing Broken Relationships

Display the pictures of the transformation tree that the small groups created in the previous session.

Return to the small groups you had in the previous meeting, where you drew a picture of the transformation tree. Looking at your trees, consider the negative outcomes that were the fruit on the tree and the beliefs that were the roots of this outcome. Discuss these two questions in your groups for the next five minutes:

• *How did broken relationships contribute to this negative result?*

• *What actions could be taken to heal these relationships?*

After the groups have discussed these questions, listen to their ideas. Be sure each group has a chance to share.

Discussion Questions

Healing Relationships

2. Our broken relationship with creation has resulted in disease from bacteria or viruses, natural disaster and famine, insects or wild animals that destroy gardens, and pollution of air and water.

3. When people reject God, they often turn to false or harmful beliefs, resulting in fear and a lack of hope.

Loving God and Loving Our Neighbors

1. We don't want to be troubled or add to our own problems; we are afraid or think we are ill-equipped to help; we lack love for others.

2. Anyone who needs help.

5. Physically—sickness or injury, lack of food or shelter, losing a job, taking drugs or alcohol, being robbed of our money and possessions; mentally—very little or no education, not taught right from wrong; emotionally—feeling inferior or fearful, lacking hope and peace, self-pity, seeing only your own problems; socially—discrimination, injustice, robbed of friends and/or family, being shunned by others in the community; good choices—peer pressure, controlled by others, not allowed to make choices, not knowing what is right, not knowing about resources that could help; spiritually—not knowing or accepting Christ, not accepting God's love and forgiveness, living in fear.

6. Shame can result from a lack of education or resources, an unfaithful spouse, a family member with a mental or physical illness, unemployment, etc.

Compassionate Neighbors

1. They are not educated; they are poor and cannot send all of their children to school; their baby died of malaria; John was beaten because of tribal differences and is lame; it is difficult for John to find work; someone stole Sarah's gardening tools; a money lender took advantage of John.

2. They believe they are cursed by their neighbors; they are afraid of the family who beat John; they do not believe God loves them; they have not accepted Jesus as their Savior; they think they are cursed and seek help from traditional healers.

3. Elizabeth and Jacob have a strong marriage and four healthy children; they attend church and believe in God; Elizabeth has learned about how to care for her family from her church.

4. Elizabeth visited Sarah and encouraged her by identifying a harmful belief and replacing it with God's truth; Elizabeth invited Sarah to attend health lessons at her church.

5. When Jacob visited John, he was friendly and respectful and did not judge John; Jacob showed compassion and encouraged John.

The Reconciling Power of Love

1. We should be devoted to and honor one another, practice hospitality, be at peace with everyone, relate to people where they are (those mourning or rejoicing), serve God with zeal, be joyful in hope, be patient in affliction, be faithful in our prayers to God, be generous, live in harmony, do what is right, hate what is evil, and do not be proud.

2. We are to bless those who mistreat us and not seek revenge; we are to live at peace with them.

3. God wants us to associate with people of low status in society, share what we have with them, and welcome them into our homes.

Session 9

Purpose: This session focuses on the important role of the church in transformational development and encourages people to think about what God expects of the church.

Helpful Hint: This session includes several questions that involve brainstorming, so encourage people to list as many different answers and examples as they can think of.

Welcome and Review

Welcome participants and share the learning objectives for today's session.

In the previous session we reviewed how God created us to live in relationships with other people, with him, and with creation. As we change through development that transforms, our relationships will also change. When we take God's truth into our hearts and believe the lesson of the good Samaritan, we will begin to change our relationships with our neighbors who are in need. Your reflection assignment in the previous session was to think of people in your community who are vulnerable or struggling because of their circumstances, and to consider reaching out to help them.

- *Who would like to share your experience in doing this?* [Allow two or three people to respond.]

If we remember that all people we meet carry within them the image of God, then we can never treat them with disdain or contempt.

- *If we are transformed by God's truths, what could we begin to do to care for the needy people in our communities?* [Link them to community and church programs that can give them information, skills, and knowledge; encourage them and help them identify their own God-given abilities; tell them of God's love for them and guide them to a deeper relationship with him.]

Poverty splits people apart, but acting with mercy brings people back together. Building strong, loving relationships can help change beliefs and actions. Remember that in our first session, the word we used for how growth happens is development. When people grow and change for the better, we call it "development." When people in whole communities begin to grow and change for the better, we often call it "community development." Also remember that in session three we talked about transformation. Transformation is the word we used for how people make positive changes in their lives. We used the picture of a tree to represent how we can make positive changes in our lives.

Discussion Questions

All Our Skills Come from God

1. The farmer's knowledge and skill come from God Almighty.

2. God gives us knowledge and skills that help us and make our lives better.

3. Every gift of knowledge, strength, and skill comes from God.

Jesus, Faith, and Works

1. To proclaim good news to the poor, freedom for the prisoners, and recovery of sight for the blind; to set the oppressed free and proclaim the year of the Lord's favor.

2. Jesus healed the sick and fed the hungry—he satisfied physical needs.

4. We are to reach out beyond the church to the people in our community.

5. People with living faith take action and serve the physical needs of their neighbors.

6. We express our love for God in our acts of love to others.

Our Roles in the Church

1. Pastors can raise congregational awareness of the needs of poor people; encourage church members to become active in caring for the poor; help to decide if and how the church should partner with other churches and organizations; provide general guidance and leadership to the ministries; lead by example— caring for the poor and needy themselves; encourage volunteers and lay leaders not to grow weary but to persist in doing good; and delegate important responsibilities to others.

2. Lay leaders help lead the day-to-day work of a ministry to the poor by planning the details and organizing people. Church members can volunteer and carry out the ministries. The entire congregation can encourage the volunteers to persevere. Everyone can pray for the work.

Session 10

Purpose: The purpose of this session is to encourage participants to reflect on all they have learned. This session also challenges them to make personal commitments to put into practice God's great commandment to love him and their neighbor by taking action in their churches and communities.

Welcome to our final session together! It has been wonderful to get to know you. We have discovered and learned many new things together. You have practiced and applied these ideas in our sessions and in your take-home assignments. Let's review some of the main points we have covered.

Helpful Hint

- Display the visual aids used in previous sessions.

Discussion Questions

Looking Back

1. Development means to grow and change over time.

2. Our physical bodies, our minds, our social relationships, our emotions and our ability to make choices. The palm of the hand represents our spiritual being which relates to God and affects and unites these various parts of ourselves.

3. Poverty is more than a lack of money. Poverty results in unmet needs in our physical, mental, emotional, and social development and undermines our ability to make good choices. People need help, love, and care in all five areas.

4. The result of Adam and Eve's sin was that sin broke relationships between God and people, between people, and with the world around them. After that, life became difficult, and poverty was common.

5. God loves us even in our sin and rebellion. God sent his son Jesus to die for our sins. God wants us to confess our sins to him, and he will forgive us our sins. If we believe in his son he will make us his own children. As his children, we are honored to be part of his church to do his will in the world.

6. Medicine, hospitals, schools, police, sunshine, rain, knowledge of how best to live.

7. Those who oppress the poor show contempt to him; they insult God who made the poor.

8. Transformation occurs when positive changes in what we believe and value align with God's truths and we see positive growth in all areas of our lives—the physical, emotional, mental, social, and how we go about making choices.

9. Our beliefs (the roots) control our values (the trunk), which then influence our actions (the branches) and determine what results (fruits) will be seen in our lives.

10. If we believe something to be true, even if it is a lie, the choices we make and our actions will reflect those beliefs. For example: If we believe that women are not equal to men, then we may decide not to educate girl children.

11. We need to be connected to Jesus to bear fruit; apart from him we can do nothing.

12. Some beliefs are not true; they are lies from Satan, the deceiver. These lies determine what we value and lead to actions that contribute to poverty and suffering.

13. We must faithfully teach and trust God's truth from his Word; we must replace harmful lies with God's truth and pray for God's power to overcome these lies.

14. We need to make sure our beliefs are based on God's truths; if not, we will be negatively affected. We cannot bear good fruit if we are not rooted in God's truths and following Jesus.

15. Churches teach God's truth to help people recognize some of the lies they have believed.

16. We need to have mercy and to care for people in need—even if they are our enemies.

17. Healthy relationships will result in less violence in families, less shunning and discrimination, more respect and love for others, and maybe even fewer wars.

People are more likely to develop in all areas of their lives when their relationships are strong.

18. God has called and directed the church to do his will in this world, and that includes caring for the poor and needy just as Jesus himself did. Because all people are created in God's image, when we help them we are honoring and serving God.

19. God has given each person in the church knowledge, skills, and gifts to be used to do his will. All are called to serve and use their gifts. The people of the congregation are one of the greatest strengths of the church.

Biblical Reflection

1. Loving God with our whole being and loving our neighbors as ourselves.

2. We cannot separate loving God from loving our neighbors. In fact, we show love for God when we love our neighbors.

3. Only God can make things grow and develop.

4. Broken relationships—between God and people, between people, and between people and creation—are a cause of suffering.

5. God loves us and wants to give us good gifts.

6. Our acts of kindness to those in need honor God.

7. We are to fight injustice and care for the needs of the poor and oppressed.

8. We must take action to care for those in need because this is an act of love to God.

9. Our words and actions are reflections of our thoughts and feelings.

10. When our lives are fruitful, it reveals our connection to God as a follower of Jesus.

11. We can remain in Jesus by learning about him and following him closely, reading our Bibles, praying, and spending time with others who follow him.

12. When our minds are renewed, our beliefs and values will be in line with all of Jesus' teaching, including how we should care for the vulnerable.

13. The renewal of our minds happens every time we turn from the lies of the world to God's truth.

14. Satan is the king of deceit, keeping people from seeing the truth and the light of God.

15. God is greater than Satan and has overcome the false spirits of this world.

16. We don't want to be troubled or add to our own problems; we are afraid or think we are ill-equipped to help; we lack love for others.

17. We are to bless those who mistreat us and not seek revenge; we are to live at peace with them. God wants us to associate with people of low status in society, share what we have with them, and welcome them into our homes.

18. When we care for those in need, God promises that he will satisfy and strengthen us.

19. Jesus came to proclaim the good news and to offer freedom and healing.

20. People with living faith take action and care for the physical needs of others.

ABOUT THE AUTHOR

Gil Odendaal, PhD, DMin, is senior vice president of integral mission at World Relief (www.worldrelief.org). From directing global initiatives for Saddleback Church to building programs for other reputable global ministries, Gil has dedicated more than thirty years to equipping and serving the church around the world to seamlessly integrate word and deed ministries that transform communities, especially through health-related initiatives. His passion for seeing Christ proclaimed where there is nearly no church and strengthening the church where it does exist has resulted in ministries on four continents and in more than a hundred countries.

Gil joined World Relief in 2012, bringing innovative ways to empower the church to serve the most vulnerable in both the Global South and North. Whether a church consists of two Christ-followers gathering in a basement in a restricted-access country or a church of twenty thousand in an open Christian country, the goal of Gil and his wife, Elmarie, is the same: to serve churches so that their gospel proclamation has social consequences as they call people to love and repentance in all areas of life. Their social involvement has evangelistic consequences as they bear witness to the transforming grace of Jesus Christ.

Prior to his present position Gil served as global director for PEACE implementation with Saddleback Church in Lake Forest, California, and as global director for the HIV/AIDS Initiative under Kay Warren, assisting and facilitating the deployment of more than ten thousand short-term missionaries. For the past eighteen years he has progressively immersed himself in community development and the church's call to integral mission focusing on the least, the lost, and the last, especially those working and living in difficult places where persecution for following Christ is par for the course. Convergence of those demographics centers on unengaged people groups. Gil regularly speaks and lectures on this topic in the United States and in global settings.

Gil has also been regional coordinator for Africa and for Russia and Eastern Europe with Medical Ambassadors International. He is currently serving on the Lausanne Movement Integral Mission Leadership Team, is vice chair for the board of Accord (Association of Christian Relief and Development Organizations), and serves as a board member for Micah Global and Pastor-in-Residence (PIR) Ministries, which provides a proven process to restore hope to "at-risk" and exited pastors by partnering with God and the church.

Gil and Elmarie were both born and raised in South Africa. They have been married for forty-one years and have three adult children and five grandchildren. Elmarie shares Gil's passions and often travels with him, where she assists him in various trainings, assessments, and research-related activities.

Contact Information:
Gil Odendaal
7 East Baltimore Street, Baltimore, MD 21202
(443) 248-7877
godendaal@wr.org

ABOUT WORLD RELIEF

World Relief is a global, Christian relief and development organization that stands with the vulnerable and partners with local churches to end the cycle of suffering, transform lives and build sustainable communities. With over seventy years of experience, World Relief has twenty-seven offices in the United States that specialize in refugee and immigration services, and works in twenty countries worldwide through disaster response, health and child development, economic development and peacebuilding.

www.worldrelief.org